THE NATURAL GOLF SWING

The

GEORGE KNUDSON

Natural Golf Swing

with Lorne Rubenstein

Illustrated by Neil Harris

M&S

Copyright © 1988 George Knudson and Lorne Rubenstein
Illustrations Copyright © 1988 Neil Harris
First published in paperback 1989

Canadian Cataloguing in Publication Data

Knudson, George, 1937-1989
  The natural golf swing

ISBN 0-7710-4534-4

1. Swing (Golf).   I. Rubenstein, Lorne.   II. Title.

GV979.S9K68 1988   796.352'3   C88-093243-0

Printed and bound in Canada

McClelland & Stewart Inc.
The Canadian Publishers
481 University Avenue
Toronto, Ontario
M5G 2E9

Contents

PREFACE

BY LORNE RUBENSTEIN

IN THE WINTER OF 1968 when I was still a teenager, I thought golf was all feel and that there was no need to learn the basics. Having achieved a fairly low handicap for a golfer who relied on feel and instinct alone, I smugly thought that nobody could teach me anything about the swing. I wasn't willing to take the time to learn the swing, of course, but that's another story. My idea of instruction was a quick tip in a golf magazine. If it didn't work, I dropped it. Can't be right, I thought.

That winter of 1968 I was very aware of what George Knudson was doing on the U.S. professional circuit. It was my custom to borrow my father's car and drive to the corner of Bathurst St. and Lawrence Ave. in Toronto every night around nine o'clock to pick up *The Globe and Mail* and check the golf news. First came the news that Knudson had won the Phoenix Open. A week later, he had won the Tucson Open. Two in a row.

I'll never forget my reaction the Sunday night I learned that George had won in Tucson. Since he was four shots from the lead heading into the last round, I figured he might finish well up in the list, but surely he wouldn't win. I drove to the corner to see where he did finish.

Unable to wait until I got home, I turned the corner, stopped the car, and turned on the interior lights. There it was. Knudson had won for the second week in a row. I was ecstatic. I didn't know George at all then, but I felt so happy for him. I also felt he'd done something worth pursuing: he had evidently gotten the best out of himself. Somehow I imagined that this was what golf was all about, and that maybe one day I too could perform to the best of my ability. George's wins gave me confidence.

But then I had to think things over. George knew the golf swing. I had often read that he was a so-called "pure swinger." Jack Nicklaus had said he had a million-dollar swing. Golfers I met around Toronto courses told me that Knudson swung the club better than anybody since Ben Hogan. They told me he'd studied it, and that he had it figured out.

Gradually, I came to accept that there was a lot more to a good golf swing than feel and instinct. You had to know what you were doing. Knudson knew.

Twenty years later, I feel fortunate to have gotten to know George well and to have written this book with him. When he first looked at my swing a decade ago on the range at Glen Abbey, he told me it wasn't bad for a left-hander. Trouble was, I swing right-handed. George has helped me understand the golf swing since then. The game is so much more enjoyable for me now.

Anybody who knows George knows that he puts his heart into everything he does. He's an inspiration to his friends and I know he'll be an inspiration to all golfers who take the time to understand the golf swing he teaches in these pages. "Golf can be fun," George says, and he means it. He's a special guy, one of a kind.

1. About This Book

PICTURE A KID hitting golf balls on a practice range. He's hitting the ball with all his strength, thrilled by the idea of going at it as hard as he can. Funny thing, though. The ball doesn't seem to go far or straight. Hitting at the ball doesn't seem to work. Keeping his eye on the ball, staring at it, and focusing on it so that he can make contact with it isn't producing very satisfying shots.

That kid was me as a twelve-year-old at the St. Charles Golf and Country Club in Winnipeg, my birthplace. I worked in the backshop there, shagged balls for the pro, Les Beaven, and practised every chance I got. Practising was my thing. It got to the point where I practised one hour for every hour I was on the course. I could hardly wait to get on the range.

Like most youngsters, I was taken with the long ball. And how do you hit the long ball? Simple. You hit the ball hard. Take that club in your hands and swing it with your hands and arms as fast as you can.

But this didn't work. I wasn't getting anywhere. There was no consistency. I'd catch the ball solidly one time and then mis-hit it so badly the next time I could feel the vibration in the shaft through my fingers and in my arms. It didn't make sense. Wasn't the idea to hit the ball? And isn't that what I was doing, trying to get the clubface squarely behind the ball at impact?

Luckily, I accidentally came across something that has informed the basis of my thinking on the swing. A giant flagpole that stood in front of the St. Charles clubhouse caught my eye as I stood on the range. It wasn't doing me any good glaring at the ball and trying to hit the thing, so I decided to focus my attention on the pole. It became my target. I immediately started making better golf swings and getting more satisfactory results.

My reasoning went like this. I had been slapping at the ball while *trying* to hit it. After I hit a shot I didn't like I'd move the ball backward or forward in my stance, figuring that maybe I wasn't catching it at the right time in my swing. Or I'd fiddle with my swing by changing the angle at which I came into the ball or messing with the way I took the club back. If it worked for a shot, I thought I had the answer. It was all trial and error and it was mostly error.

My main mistake was that I had made the ball the most important consideration. The ball was everything; that's where I directed my concentration and energy. But it kept me from making a swing. I was hitting *at* the ball, not through it. I wasn't making a swing. I was chopping at the ball, cutting myself off.

I needed something to take my eye and mind *off* the ball. The flagpole was perfect for that purpose.

The flagpole became my target. So what if it was about five hundred yards away from where I stood on the practice tee? That was the point. I couldn't make the ball go that far, but I could focus on a point well beyond the ball. As I look back on my thirty-five years or so of thinking about the swing, I realize that the flagpole at St. Charles had everything to do with the development of my thoughts on golf as a target game and on the swing as a motion. The flagpole became my target, not the ball.

I exchanged the idea of hitting the ball for the idea of swinging through it toward a target.

The idea was to swing in such a way that the ball would reach the apex of its flight just as it was in front of the pole, and then blot out the pole as it fell to the ground. This picture appealed to me; I loved the idea of the ball soaring into the sky, reaching its high point, and then falling to the ground down the line of the pole. I started the swing with my hands, but at least I was swinging beyond the ball.

I didn't know it at the time, but I probably learned more about the golf swing from using that flagpole than anything that came later. It was the foundation of my conviction that golf is a game of motion directed toward a target. The ball just gets in the way. So my attention started going beyond the ball. And that's where it still is. I began to see that the ball should be in the same place in my stance every time if I were going to make a motion through it. That would promote consistency. This all pointed to a constant ball location, though I wasn't as clear on this back in my early days at St. Charles.

But the flagpole helped me think of the swing as a pure, uninterrupted, and uninhibited move in which I would have no sensation of a hit. It was as if I were studying karate or one of the other martial arts. I wanted to move *through* the target. I wanted to freewheel. Why should I let the ball stop the motion? Why should I let it interrupt the flow of my swing? I still feel this way. It's just that I've spent the last thirty-five years refining the idea of the swing as a natural motion.

Most golfers play the game as if it requires the same considerable hand-eye coordination as found in baseball, tennis, or squash. They focus on the ball and devise ways of making contact, as if golf were basically a matter of hitting the ball. By thinking this way golfers turn the game into a hand-eye game, a hit-the-ball game. But it's not.

GOLF IS A STATIONARY BALL GAME

Golf is a stationary ball game in which we make a motion toward a target. The ball simply gets in the way of the motion. That's why a golfer who is properly set up to the ball and his target can make good shots while closing his eyes. I know; during an experiment I once shot 67 at Glen Abbey, the home of the Canadian Open, while closing my eyes on each swing.

Why can blind people golf, and often quite well? It's because the ball sits still. They don't have to react to it. An assistant or coach helps the blind golfer set up to the ball. Once he has done so, he can hit the ball quite easily. He's in a good starting position in which he is oriented toward his target. He knows he wants to swing toward that target and senses that he wants to finish his swing motion facing his target. So all he needs to do is find a means of connecting the starting position to the finishing position. I'll show you how to do that.

The fact that the golf ball is stationary leads golfers to believe they must find a way to *hit* it, to get it moving. Golfers who think this way make the game more difficult than it needs to be. They out-think themselves when standing over the ball. They believe they must *make* a swing happen. It's as if they say: ''I'm going to find a way to hit that thing, if it takes my whole life.''

This attitude makes for frustrated golfers. They will study instruction book after instruction book and take series of lessons after series of lessons. Today's frustrated golfers will buy instructional videos and watch them until all hours, hoping to find the secret. I've heard of one

fellow who tapes the swings of all the great players, inserts images of his own swing next to each, and then compares his moves to theirs. I guess he figures he'll pick up something that will help him play the game he thinks he should be playing. He goes from tip to tip and theory to theory trying to find a better way to hit the ball. The only trouble is, golf is not a hit-the-ball game.

I believe that golf involves a swing motion directed toward a target. Moreover, it's a whole-body motion. We don't hit at the ball, rather, we swing a unit – our hands, arms, and club – indeed, our whole body, *through the ball toward our target*. We focus on the target. The ball simply gets in the way of the clubhead as we swing through it. We find a location for our bodies relative to the ball so that we can make contact with the ball as we swing toward the target. If the ball is in the right location, we'll get it every time along the way. The ball will sit in the path of the clubhead. We won't need to control the club or force it on track. We'll let it track. We won't need to interfere with the golf club.

Golf is a target game, and we should direct all our efforts toward making a swing motion toward the target while letting our bodies travel freely. The golfer's task is to find a repetitive motion so that the clubhead will send the ball to the target while taking him along to a finishing position in which he is in balance. He needs to find a means of connecting the starting position to the finishing position. I'll teach the means of doing so in this book.

I refer to the swing as a motion. We ignore the ball. As I say, it simply gets in the way of the motion. The motion connects the starting position to the finishing position. We design the starting position so that we have the best chance of making a motion toward the target and we design the finishing position so that at the end of the motion we face the target. The club simply travels as it will, carried along by centrifugal force and inertia, the laws of motion that govern all physical activity.

THE LAWS
ARE THERE ALREADY.
THEY'RE PART OF YOU

When we understand that golf is a target game, we can more readily conceive of a "natural" swing; natural because as a motion it is ruled by the aforementioned laws of motion. in the following pages I'll show you how to make a swing motion based upon these fundamental laws. The motion will enable you to turn golf into a most pleasurable physical experience. And you won't have to do anything consciously in order to use the laws once you understand the fundamentals of the natural swing. The laws are there already; they're part of nature, part of you. I'll show you how to *let* them operate, how not to interfere with them. I'll explore with you all the ways in which golf is a "passive" game, one in which we *let* most things happen rather than *make* them happen. You'll learn these involuntary or automatic aspects of the motion (they tend to be positions during the swing that most golfers think they must create). There are indeed a few voluntary actions that you must learn, but they simply get you in motion. They have nothing to do with putting yourself into a position during the motion. If you start in a good position and finish in a good position not much can go wrong in between. I'll show you why.

How many times have you played a round of golf while thinking of who knows how many different things to do during your swing? And how many times have you been so thoroughly exasperated that on the last tee you finally said: "The hell with all these tips and ideas. I'm just going to set up properly and swing toward my target." I'll bet it's at that point that you've often hit your finest shot. I call it the "come-back-tomorrow" shot, or the "what-time-do-we-play-tomorrow?" shot.

GIVE UP CONTROL TO GAIN CONTROL

So what happened then? How did you suddenly make your best swing? Very simply, you gave up control. You stopped trying to manipulate the clubhead and hit the ball. You forgot about doing this and that during the swing.

Maybe you visualized a full swing, maybe you thought only of rhythm, or maybe you thought only of swinging through to your target. Or maybe you didn't think of a thing. The point is that *you gave up control and the result was that you gained control.* You stopped thinking about what to do with the club and let it flow on its own. You connected a starting position to a finishing position. The club went along on a pure path and you went along for the ride. You let centrifugal force and inertia work.

I remember the first time I felt centrifugal force and inertia (centrifugal force is the outward force acting on a body that is rotating in a circle around a central point; inertia is the property by which matter continues in its existing state of rest or uniform motion unless that state is changed by external force). The effect generated a powerful and accurate swing, yet I hadn't a thing to do with it except allow it to happen. All I did was set myself in motion.

Until then, I'd only had glimpses of a pure swing. I'd thought I had *to do* so much to swing a golf club, but suddenly in one swing I felt like the golf club had swung itself. There was no resistance. I sensed that the club was travelling on a pure, undisturbed path, and that I wasn't doing a thing consciously with my hands and arms to take it there. It was a feeling of totally letting go. It felt wonderful.

Having experienced how fluid and pleasurable the swing could be, I naturally wanted to repeat it every time. But like the golfer who makes that exciting "come-back-tomorrow" shot, I knew I couldn't depend on my feelings to bring it back. I needed to understand what had happened that time. And so began a personal quest for a conception of the swing that would best allow the force to operate. It took me some fifteen years to fully understand it all and another ten to feel I really knew how to communicate it to people. All along I was using a natural motion, but I needed to understand it as such. Now that I do, I can give you the benefit of my studies. The golf swing is not at all difficult; you'll find that once you understand the conception of the swing as a natural motion, you'll make rapid progress.

There's no need for you to suffer on the course. Golf can be a real joy. But you need to understand what you are trying to do. You cannot change effectively unless you have a clear image of what you are trying to do.

THE "IMPERSONAL" SWING

The golf swing that I advocate is an impersonal swing. We are all trying to accomplish the same objectives: create direction, distance, and trajectory. If the laws of motion are operative, and they must be, then it follows that we should be able to find a way to accomplish these objectives that is independent of the idiosyncracies of each and every golfer. This isn't to say that my swing won't look different than yours, or yours from the next guy's. We are all shaped differently, and so our swings will vary in shape and appearance. You're taller or shorter, more or less flexible, or heavier or lighter than the next fellow. But you're also the exact same being: you have a body which we can perceive as a machine. And we want to put this body in the service of meeting the objectives of the game.

The most efficient way of doing this is to create a swing motion in which balance is the bedrock fundamental. We do nothing in the natural swing that is at the expense of balance, since disturbing balance will lead to a loss of control and power. Everything I will say in this book is based on balance. I won't ask you to do a thing that disturbs balance. The balanced swing is the most satisfying swing. It's also the most logical and simplest swing that will get the job done.

A word about the title of this book: *The Natural Golf Swing*. If something is natural, why do we have to learn it?

Bear in mind that walking and talking are natural, but we did have to learn these skills. We learned them over a period of time, even though we didn't know what we were learning, or even that we *were* learning. Gradually it became natural for us to walk and talk. Those of us who have learned another language as adults have had to learn a new vocabulary along with the rules or fundamentals of

the language, its grammar. The same goes for, say, ice-skating or dancing. We learn the grammar of these motions before we can do them without thinking.

Most golfers speak a language without knowing the vocabulary or the grammar. Golf, as I've said, is not a hand-eye, hit-the-ball game. Strike these phrases from your golf vocabulary. Replace them with words such as target and motion.

I say that golfers don't know the vocabulary or grammar for one reason: I've been there. I was in the same position for too long. It didn't matter where I was – Canada, the U.S., Japan, or the U.K. – I heard the same ideas you've heard, tried every gimmick you've tried, and probably more. I struggled for the first fifteen years of my career to find a swing that I could be sure would work when it mattered most, while I contended for championships.

It took me those fifteen years of observation and thinking and playing to begin to understand the logic behind the swing. And only after this last decade of teaching – I left the tour in the late 1970s to teach – have I come to see that the swing does not have to be complicated, as long as we appreciate that the logical swing is in fact the swing that is the most easily repeatable. This swing is a natural swing in the sense that it's governed by basic laws of nature.

You have exactly what you need to learn the swing I'll show you. You won't need to manufacture a thing. I'm going to teach you a way to swing that has nothing to do with *making anything happen*. But it will have everything to do with *letting things happen*. There's nothing fancy or complicated about it. If I can do it, anybody can. I mean this. I'm no different than you.

Think of it. I'm not a fabulous physical specimen. Nor was I born with a flair for golf. But I know that the golf swing is so much easier and more enjoyable than you think it is. I know this because I've been through the same theories you have. I bought every misconception, tried them all. But my studies eventually took me to the point where I realized the swing is natural. It can be graceful.

GOLF FOR RELAXATION

Golf is a physical activity for relaxation. I don't see how a golfer can be relaxed if he clutters his mind with ideas of where to put his elbows on the backswing, or what to do with his hands when he comes through the ball. This is the old paralysis by analysis that we're all too familiar with. We make ourselves crazy when we think so much. As far as relaxing goes, forget it. Who can relax when he's so mixed up? Who can relax when he figures he's found the answer on one swing, only to top or snap-hook the next shot?

If golf is a physical activity for relaxation, then we might try to find a swing motion that will encourage relaxation. But most golfers look like they're in straitjackets. There's no freedom or ease of motion.

It hurts me to see the way most golfers approach the game. I don't think it's right that you should be so frustrated. That's why I'd like to introduce you to a new game in which balance is the number one key.

I'm not going to tell you what's wrong with your current swing. I couldn't anyway, since

I can't see you. But frankly, I don't care what's wrong with your swing. I don't work with what people have. I work with what they can be. And so I ask only that you drop what you have. Let it go. Put everything that you have heard aside. Take a fresh look at the swing.

Once you've learned the natural golf swing, you will be in position to understand, appreciate, and even enjoy every shot you play, including those that don't come off as you wish. You'll be able to evaluate any one shot because you'll understand the factors that go into the successful swing motion. You will progress from being concerned with the result of a shot to being absorbed in the process of swinging. You'll learn that what matters isn't what you do on any one shot, but what you are attempting to do. You'll be taking the long-range view.

In the next chapter, I will present the way I learned the natural swing. I'll discuss the general theory of the natural swing in chapter three, while balance in all its aspects will take up chapter four. Chapters five through eight will present the motion itself: the starting form; the loading, or backswing motion; the unloading, or downswing motion; and the finishing form. In chapter nine, I'll discuss all the misconceptions we've bought that have kept us from the natural swing, while in chapter ten I'll present a series of drills for practising the segments of the motion. In chapter eleven, I'll review the natural swing motion from a particular point of view. There's a glossary at the end of the book to which you can refer to familiarize yourself with the terms I'll use in the book.

We can get so much out of golf. I know I have, and I'd like to see the same for you. Golf is the game of a lifetime, one in which you can get better and better.

2. My Learning Process

ALTHOUGH this is a book about letting yourself play golf naturally, in some ways it's odd that I should be writing it. I originally thought that the mechanics of the swing were what really counted, and that all I had to do was learn the parts. Fortunately, I also felt that if I were going to incorporate anything into my swing, it had to be logical. In the end, I rejected the illogical for the logical, the unnatural for the natural. It was just the way I looked at golf. But it took me fifteen years to become a "natural."

The atmosphere at St. Charles Golf and Country Club, where I began around 1948 (I was born in Winnipeg in 1937), was conducive to my inquisitive mind. At least half a dozen guys who worked on staff were good players and strong competitors, and we all worked seriously on our games. The pro, Les Beaven, was also very talented and, more importantly, he encouraged the juniors. Then there were Al Nelson, Len Collett and Len Harvey, who won the 1953 and 1954 Manitoba Opens. Both Collett and Harvey are pros now, as is Jimmy Collins, another capable St. Charles player who went on to become the pro there. He's still there. I watched these guys and became passionate about golf right from the beginning. I knew I had to work at it to compete in such a crowd.

None of us enjoyed losing. We really pushed one another.

My attitude was that I would succeed through technique. I wanted to minimize the influence of luck, to get to the point where I was secure about what I was doing. None of this "here-today, gone-tomorrow" business. I wanted some security. Even today I don't know how people who play the game for a living manage without being certain of their methods. I knew I couldn't live that way. So I looked for something that made sense.

At first, I imitated Beaven and others around the club. It was just kid's play, but I did get a sense of the rhythm of the swing. Not that I had any idea as to what caused rhythm, or even what made the ball fly one way or another. Still, I really liked the whole idea of being able to control the flight of the ball one day. When I was thirteen, I shot 86 in the first junior tournament I played. That won my division; kind of neat, I thought.

A NEW GRIP

Just after that tournament, I learned about a new-style grip the pros were teaching in Florida. Herb Quinn, an older member at St. Charles, had picked it up down south. Until Herb talked to me I'd thought the standard grip was where the V's formed by the index finger and thumb of both hands went to the right shoulder. But he shocked me when he said, "No, son, they've got their hands on where they're opposing one another. The thumbs are on top of the shaft and the palms face one another."

This was a revelation to me. It meant that the way everybody was gripping the club wasn't necessarily correct. It also meant that not everything was known about the swing. I suppose I should have realized this even as a kid, but I was then in my imitation stage. After I began to think about this new grip, I realized what was important; the former grip really didn't make sense. Why would you want to hold the club with the V's pointing to the right shoulder? I sensed that this would force you to

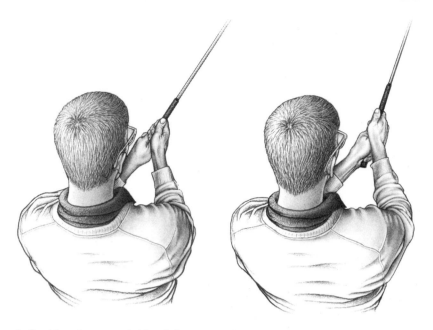

Left, old and unacceptable; *right*, new and acceptable.

compensate during the swing if you were going to put the club-head square on the ball. The most logical grip was hands-opposing, just as in prayer. As a thirteen-year-old, I didn't understand how important this was to the development of a sound and sensible golf swing, but I'm glad I learned it early. I guess I figured that the best way was the most natural way. I let my arms hang in front of me with my palms opposing, so why not grip the club that way? Later, I realized that this was the centre-piece of the starting form; it represented a balanced means of holding the club. Ignore it and you can't help but go wrong. The proper grip, though, is a fine means of assuring a balanced form.

Herb Quinn's advice excited me. I realized there was more to golf than just hitting the ball. There were reasons things happened. He was a great old guy, about seventy then, and had seen plenty of ideas come and go. This one seemed worthwhile, and I've stuck with it since.

I soon became serious about practising and began to love my time on the range. After we got through our work around the range and shop, the boss would tell us to go play. I'd tell the fellows to go ahead and that I'd meet them after nine. I wanted to practise for the hour and fifteen minutes it would take them to play nine holes and I'd join them on the back side.

As much as I loved golf and was fascinated by the swing, I really didn't give any thought to playing the game for a living until I saw the 1952 Canadian Open at St. Charles. That's when I decided I'd like to turn pro. After the tournament, I told my folks that that's what I wanted. I was lucky. They encouraged me right away. So did Les Beaven. My folks said: "If that's what you want, go for it. Just don't come crying if things don't work out."

A kid couldn't ask for more support. My folks knew how much I enjoyed the game and that it's good for a kid to go after what he wants. So what if you fail? Go for it. That was their attitude. Because of them I feel the same way. That's how I teach. It's not what you do that counts, but what you attempt to do. Get into every shot; that's the pleasure of the game.

Hooked as I was on golf, I wanted to learn everything I could about the swing. Ben Hogan's *Power Golf* was one of the first books I read. In it he talks about a "lateral shift," where the golfer is supposed to whip his hips through the ball and around to the left. I tried it, but it didn't work for me. Maybe it hurt too much. I didn't want anything in my swing that hurt. I wanted the swing to feel good. Or maybe I misunderstood the material. That commonly happens when one golfer reads about how another one swings. It's the problem of the golf swing being perceived as a personal swing. I think about the lateral shift today and wonder how I didn't break my back trying it. Still, that was part of my experimentation.

One of the aspects I enjoyed most about golf was that I could be alone on the range or course. I spent hours out there trying to figure things out. Lots of people who love golf also thrive on being on their own. That was my nature. But I wasn't only pounding balls; I was observing, asking questions.

As a youngster, I never seemed to catch the ball with the inlay on the driver when I set the middle of the clubface right behind the ball. I kept on catching the ball on the heel of the club, breaking the wood on the heel side of the insert. It annoyed me. I'd hit these ugly little shots, and I had trouble figuring out why.

Setting the toe of the club to the ball to allow the clubhead to pull out.

One day, I decided to try to catch the ball way out on the toe of the driver. I set up the ball on the toe and figured that's where I would make contact. It wasn't the sweet spot, but setting the ball up on the sweet spot hadn't been doing me any good either. So what happens? I hit this thing and it flies off the club like a rocket compared to what I'd been doing.

That got me thinking. "If I set the ball up on the toe, does it ever go." I didn't realize I was contacting it right in the middle of the clubhead. I'd been trying to hit the ball after setting it up on the inlay and had been smacking it on the heel. That's why the wood was chipped. But suddenly, after setting the ball up on the toe, the ball was coming off the face solidly. I decided that the clubhead must be pulling out, and accepted that.

It seems like such subtle stuff when I look back on it now, but I can see that I was struggling toward a conception of the swing that relied on natural laws. I guess I could have missed it all or tried to control what was happening. It didn't seem logical to some people that you'd set the ball up on the toe of the club if you wanted to catch it in the middle of the face. But I didn't fight it. I learned to make the adjustment. Maybe it was because I was a fairly little guy then. I didn't want to overpower the game since I didn't think I could. So the easiest way was to sit back and let it happen.

Weighing one hundred and nothing, it was easy for me to let the club take over. It felt like a substantial mass.

THE EFFECT OF CENTRIFUGAL FORCE

I didn't know that I was suddenly catching the ball in the centre of the clubface because of the centrifugal force that was pulling the clubhead out and down. But that was the case. Eventually, I learned that centrifugal force is one of the laws of motion that enable us to make a natural swing. It's behind that wonderful feeling we get when we swing seemingly without effort and then see the ball flying far and straight. Centrifugal force is also a terrific means of achieving a maximum swing arc, or extension. No wonder it became one of the principal ideas behind my concept of the swing.

It also encouraged me to continue looking at things my own way. Not that I was all that sure about what was happening, or what conclusions I might come to. I was still observing with a teenager's eye, eagerly, but not critically. Nevertheless, these experiences were the beginning of my study.

I also observed other golfers. It was exciting to see the U.S. pros in the '52 Canadian Open, all right, but I soon learned we also had a hell of a lot of talent at home. At first, I was only aware of Stan Leonard and Al Balding, but it didn't take long to notice guys like Lyle Crawford and Moe Norman. I played against them in the 1954 Canadian Amateur and the next year in Calgary, when I won the Canadian Junior. These guys could play, but I didn't see any reason I couldn't do as well or better, especially if I could figure out the swing. I quit school to pursue that goal.

After deciding that golf was it for me, I didn't see any reason to continue in school. I needed to learn out on the range and the course and the tour. So in 1957, when I was still an amateur, I caddied the winter tour. I worked for Balding and Leonard and spent every extra minute watching players. What were they made of? What did the top players have in common?

Ben Hogan was on tour at the time. He'd nearly been killed in an auto accident in February, 1949 when he and his wife Valerie were hit by a Greyhound bus during a fog in western Texas. Nobody believed he would ever golf again; most people figured he wouldn't even walk. But not Hogan. He had to recover from a double fracture of the pelvis, a fractured collarbone, a broken inner bone in his right ankle, and a broken right rib. Yet he came back better than ever. He won three U.S. Opens, two Masters, and one British Open after his accident. This had all happened by 1953, but in 1957 he was still the most precise golfer on tour. He's still regarded as the most accurate player ever. I was fascinated with the man. I watched him every chance I could.

SEEING HOGAN FOR THE FIRST TIME

I'll never forget the first time I set eyes on Hogan. I was nineteen, and had read that Hogan was going to play in a pro-am in Los Angeles. I knew I had to see this man play, so I went down there – and Hogan wasn't even playing. It didn't matter, because now I was determined to find him, and I did later that year at the Bing Crosby National Pro-Am, better known as the "Crosby," in Pebble Beach, California.

Hogan was playing Cypress Point, my favourite course, along with Jimmy Demaret, Bing Crosby, and Bob Hope. If I had one round left in my life, I'd play Cypress at 7:15 in the morning when the fog was still in. I can still see the setting on the first tee. The fog is so thick that I can't see the cypress tree that's down there 240 yards on the right side, but I know it's there. As I walk down the hill to my second shot, I'm looking up through the fog and I can see the sunlight and the green. I'm in heaven. And it never lets up until you get to the clubhouse. This is the kind of place where I first saw Ben Hogan.

He didn't disappoint me. Hogan was playing the fourteenth when I saw him. I caught him hitting his second shot and he put it in about six feet from the hole. The fourteenth happens to be one of the most gorgeous holes in the world to run into anybody, never mind Hogan. Anyway, it all started with that shot: I was quickly hooked on the way Hogan went about being a golfer. On the next hole, a three-par, he knocks it stiff and makes two. At the sixteenth, that stunning hole across the bay to a green surrounded by rocks and ocean, he hits a three-wood on the front of the green and chips in for another birdie.

Hogan had no fear as he stood on the tee at the sixteenth. It was just another shot. No anxiety; what a hole to be cool on. If you ever want to find out what kind of control you have, how anxious you are, walking to the sixteenth tee at Cypress will tell you. You're shooting at this green 215 yards away and, surrounded by ocean, it looks like you're shooting to a tabletop. With the wind conditions, it didn't take long to find out who was secure and who wasn't. People walk to that tee and you can almost hear their hearts pounding in anticipation. Most guys are such wrecks by the time they get there they can't even lay up. Not Hogan, though. He had proper procedures, which make it just another golf shot from point A to point B. Develop the right procedures and the environment won't bother you. People can get themselves in such a negative state because of the conditions. That's when the golf course plays *them*.

At the seventeenth, Hogan sticks it in there fifteen feet. Birdie again. At the eighteenth, he hits it eight feet and hangs the putt on the lip. I think, ''Hmmm, that's Hogan.'' From that day on, every opportunity I had to watch Hogan, I'd drop my clubs and observe him. I knew I could learn a lot just sitting there quietly: I was watching the maestro. He made it look so routine all the time. He knew where the ball was going every swing. The other golfers had it sometimes and lost it at other times. Their games depended on their moods, their feel that day. Not Hogan. He had something nobody else had. When he set up over the ball, he knew the shot was going to come off. You knew it. Everybody knew it. And I wanted the same feeling, the same certainty. What did Hogan have that was unique?

I didn't find out right away. At first I looked for the common factors between Hogan, Sam Snead, Jimmy Demaret, Jackie Burke, Lionel and Jay Hebert, Dick Mayer, and Tommy Bolt. There was a great bunch on tour then. I used to spend all day watching golf swings: the guys I've mentioned, and Ted Kroll, Julius Boros, Lloyd Mangrum, Cary Middlecoff, Ken Venturi, Billy Maxwell, Gene Littler, Art Wall, and Don January. These fellows were my teachers. The practice field was my classroom.

What a place to be, with a wonderful crowd like that. I spent more hours sitting on the range watching the fellows than I did caddying. I looked and I looked at all these personal swings and finally I noticed one important element: every player who struck the ball well maintained the same firmness in his left wrist at the completion of the swing as he had in the starting position. His form at the finish was the same as at the start. When I discovered this, I discovered a gem. Wall did it about as well as anybody – as strange as his swing was with that ten-finger, baseball grip. Same thing with Boros. He's as good as I've ever seen in terms of natural form. The wrist didn't break down. There was none of what Bolt liked to call ''flippy-wristed kids' stuff.'' And January: he was so supple and took the club back so far. But he was always in balance. He was just that flexible.

These fellows interested me. There had to be a reason the best golfers in the world had some elements in common. I was especially interested in that one common factor that stood out: the way the guys maintained the same hand-wrist formation at the end of the swing as at the beginning. But I couldn't figure out how they did it. Naive as I was, I tried to imitate them. But I couldn't even come close to it. I tried to force my left wrist to stay firm through the completion of the swing. But, since my swing at the time was all upper-body – all hands and arms – that was the only way I thought I could accomplish the move.

I had no idea that the only way
to maintain a firm left wrist was
to use my legs, to transfer weight
going back and through. My
legs, however, moved very little
then. I didn't pay much attention
to footwork. The reason? I was
stuck on one of golf's number
one misconceptions: keep the
head still. I tried to keep my
head still and I couldn't move.
The only way I could get the
club back was with my hands
and arms.

The Classroom: observing (*left to
right*) Ken Venturi, Ben Hogan, Sam
Snead, and Julius Boros.

The hands and wrists are in the same formation at the start and finish.

THE IMPORTANCE OF THE LEGS

It didn't take long to realize that it was far better to let my legs lead the downswing. Then there isn't any restriction. The wrist won't collapse. It's pulled along by the leg drive. Otherwise

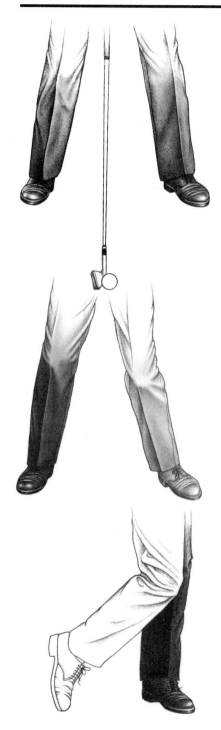

you're just flapping your arms and the wrist collapses. Poor shots result; you can't get power or direction unless the left wrist is firm throughout. Neither can you maintain the hands and wrist in the same formation as at the start. That's why you want to start the downswing with the legs.

The hands just flip over when there's a resistance. You've got to get the legs moving. This also keeps the hands quiet, or "passive," as I prefer to say. Passive hands simply mean that we do nothing consciously with the hands during the swing. I didn't begin to appreciate what this meant for consistency until I started using my legs. My hands now began to just go along for the ride, to hang on to the club.

Think about it. When you walk, you're transferring weight all the time, back and forth, to and fro. The same thing happens in the golf swing; we move away from the ball on our backswing and our weight transfers to our right side. We move through the

Top, start, equal weight distribution; *centre*, loading, 75%-25% *bottom*, unloading, 0-100%.

ball to our target and our weight transfers to our left side. If we swing with our hands and arms alone, we're swinging with less than a full deck. And we're setting up restrictions and inhibitions. But we want to develop a natural, uninhibited swing motion. We want total freedom of movement. How can we have that when our legs are rooted to the ground like tree stumps? Move the legs and the rest of the body moves. Footwork is so important.

After I began to understand weight transfer and the importance of the legs in the swing, I ran into Harvey Penick. Penick is one of the great teachers of all time. All the golfers I admire have talked with him over the years and listened carefully to what he has to say: the list includes Byron Nelson, Ben Hogan, Mickey Wright, Louise Suggs, and Patty Berg. Now Penick told me: "Son, if you're going to play this game for a living, you'd better learn how to use your legs."

Penick's advice confirmed what I'd noticed on the range. And so I began to work on getting my legs into my swing. It wasn't easy; I had some bad habits to overcome.

I'd had a problem as a kid with balance. Because I used my hands as much as I did, I tended to drift. I was a bit of a flailer as I manipulated the clubhead so that I could get it on the ball. But I didn't need to do that. Instead, I got my legs involved, and by doing so, I was able to eliminate some of the excess hand action. Now that my body was moving, my hands simply worked on their own. I didn't have to do a thing with them, and what a relief that was. Like everybody else, I'd been seeing hand action while watching golfers. But I was seeing it wrong. It was poor observation on my part.

Hand action is a result of the swing put in its proper form: what I call a "by-the-way-happening," an involuntary action. It's the legs that carry the arms and hands. The arms and hands merely go along for a free ride. This insight introduced much

Load, 75%-25%; start, 50%-50%; unload, 0-100%.

more consistency into my game. I learned that weight transfer is the means of moving the hands, arms, and clubhead.

Still, my balance wasn't what it could be. I knew that if I was ever going to play to my potential I would need better balance. But how could I achieve it? I came back on the winter tour in 1958 to play as an amateur, then played as a pro in 1959 and 1960. I was in school, observing every minute I could.

The range was my classroom, Hogan my main teacher. I still hadn't figured the guy out. He looked so different. His shots had more character and he knew where the hole was. But it took a while to grasp the key: he had better *balance* than any golfer.

Hogan was so stable over the ball and throughout the swing. He looked so solid, and yet he also gave it everything he had.

Hogan had a controlled and powerful golf swing and balance was the key. It looked to me that if you hit him anywhere, you'd be hitting something dead solid. He never looked wobbly. As for me, I wasn't falling over, but I was continually rolling over onto the outside of my left foot and left heel. So was everybody else. Everybody except Hogan, that is. He was dead solid flat on his left foot at the finish of his swing.

The thing that Hogan did differently to stay in balance was really quite elementary. He took a wider stance than the others. When he set up over the ball, he pointed his left foot out about a quarter-turn to the left and set it outside his left shoulder. This gave him a boxer's stance; he was in a "go" position. He was ready to give it a whack with his whole body. By setting his left foot beyond his shoulder, he ensured that he wouldn't roll over onto his foot and heel.

Finish positions emphasizing foot locations.

Having gained at least some appreciation of the fact that the elements of the golf swing came together in a unified manner, I tried to incorporate what I'd learned into my swing. As I said, Hogan was my model. Before long, people were saying I looked more like Hogan than Hogan himself. I took that as a great compliment, but I was still a long way off from being the "natural" people thought I was. And I wanted to be a "natural"; I wanted to feel good over the ball and during the swing. But I was contriving the whole thing. I still didn't have a full understanding of what it meant to *let* myself swing. I was still trying to do things. I was still *making* the swing happen. I was using too much effort, *trying* too hard. I felt that I was over-exerting myself. Rather than simplifying the swing and eliminating moves, I was adding to it. And it was work. It took me a year and a half to achieve the balanced position at the finish that I so admired in Hogan.

A BREAKTHROUGH

It wasn't until the summer of 1960 that I had a breakthrough in my understanding. I had come to Toronto's Oakdale Golf and Country Club in 1958 as an assistant to Bill Hamilton, who later went on to become the executive director of the Canadian Professional Golfers Association. Oakdale was a terrific place for me; the members knew I wanted to play the game professionally rather than work at a club. They let me hit balls and play as much as I wanted. It was during one of my practice sessions that it occurred to me that the golf swing had to be impersonal. If it followed the laws of physical motion, then we were all trying to do the same thing. The idea that golf was an individual game had led us to believe every swing was different and that we had to find our own ways, each and every one of us. That summer

The head goes where the body carries it.

day at Oakdale I asked myself: "What would the swing look like if I cut my head off? What would it look like if I were a machine, if I were designing a machine to create a golf swing?"

First, I realized that the head had nothing to do with the swing. If we were searching for a natural swing, the head had to go where the body carried it. The idea of keeping the head still suddenly made no sense to me. How could I swing back from the ball and through it without my head moving along?

Allowing the head to move helped me realize that the head had no purpose in the golf swing. It would simply go where it wanted. It struck me that trying to keep the head still was unnatural. It also caused so many problems: poor balance, keeping the weight forward while moving back, picking the club up, and that reverse C position so many golfers fall into at the finish of their swings and that hurts their backs. (I'll have more to say on this later.) So, as I said, I had one of those "aha!" experiences at Oakdale. Now I was going to put the swing into the form it best functions in. I was going to develop an impersonal swing.

Until 1960, I had learned so much, good and bad, from other people. I didn't necessarily accept their ideas as the be-all and end-all, but I was curious and I'd experiment if I thought the ideas made sense. Logic was the deciding factor. I'd observed other players for a few years and was able to put things together in a reasonable fashion. It started with the grip and it ended with balance. I had persevered until I got it. I wasn't going to let up until I had some answers. I was like a kid with his Lego blocks: pick up a piece here, add another there. I'd use what seemed logical. I was fitting pieces of a puzzle together, but I had to continually think about the pieces. I still didn't feel I could perform the motion without contriving it. I still didn't know that the natural swing was the one where you set up the motion at address and let it happen, by design.

I first felt that the swing must be impersonal just prior to going on tour in 1961. In the meantime, I'd won only one cheque in my first three years on tour – for a hundred dollars in the Crosby when I made the cut. But I didn't care. I was learning. I'd come home and my head was full of things to work on. I may not have been making any money, but so what? This was a learning process. I was going to school and I had to go through it. I wasn't at all discouraged. It gave me something to work with. That's why I played so well in Canada. I had all kinds of motivation to get at it when I came home.

I didn't lose very often at home. It wasn't that I was that terrific a golfer or that I had any particular gift for the game. But I'd done my homework and was more knowledgeable than others. I kept saying, "Look at me, I'm nothing special." There must have been something in my head that made sense. I had a passion to understand the why, the causes of good golf shots.

Still, I felt the tension in those early years. I was playing to make a living, but my real intent was to practise. That's how I felt. I needed to practise to improve, yet I had to make a living. So I had to play with what I had at the time. I didn't want to start changing while I was playing.

By 1960, I had practised for some ten years. Sure, I was winning Canadian tournaments and making a living, but I still wasn't good enough for where I wanted to go: as far as my potential would carry me, the big leagues, world-class. I wasn't going to make it the way I was going at it. I could accept that I was better than the next guy, but I felt forced and restricted – it was work, not fun. And I didn't like the idea that I had to hold myself in to get the job done. Had I stuck with that approach I never would have succeeded. I'd have become rigid with anxiety.

I knew what the swing was about. I knew that I had to develop a pure, undisturbed plane – the path the clubhead travels on – and to maximize an arc, the perimeter or outer boundary of the plane. In both cases, I knew that I wanted them the same every time. That's what Hogan had, and it meant consistency. You could live with consistency.

I also felt that I would be more consistent if I could keep the clubhead from fluttering during the swing. I would feel more secure if I knew where it was, if I weren't flipping it around. So I had arrived at the notion of passive hands, where the hands do nothing but hold on to the club during the swing. They move only because the lower body moves; we begin the swing with our weight shifting to our back foot and finish it with our weight totally on our forward foot. The hands and arms and the clubhead move in response to our footwork.

So I knew all that, and then in 1960 at Oakdale I had asked, "Okay, what form do you put this thing in?"

I had said to myself, "It's a machine. It hasn't got a head. What form will you put it in to make it create a perfect plane and to maximize an arc?" I knew I could build a machine with the same capabilities as those I was striving for. And so I decided what the form had to be. I knew the function. I knew what I wanted to create: plane, arc, source of power, variance in trajectory, distance, direction, and curvature. I worked with these thoughts.

Until then, I was trying this and that, and living with the result. If I got a good result, I felt okay. But it was an empty feeling because I couldn't be sure of what was causing it. I had ideas, but no overall picture. I realized I had to know exactly what it was and what had to be done to have it happen time and time again. Then I would learn to vary the characteristics of the shot with minor alterations to the form. I knew it could be done. Yes, it could happen.

The process I used was to find a form in which I didn't have to worry about my arms, hands, and the club. The motor is the body. I'm talking about a whole body swing. The head, as I say, went along for the ride. The feet became the pivot points; back to the right foot, through to the left. I started using them.

I'd never have come across this if I hadn't asked the question about what I'd want if I cut my head off. "Let's make this thing impersonal." That was the best approach I could have taken to the problem of creating a repeating swing.

The consequence of this was that when I went out in 1961, I finally felt I did have some answers. I'd learned that distance comes from the pace at which we transfer weight; that is, the faster I move from my back foot toward my front foot, the more clubhead speed I'll generate.
I also understood that I could vary trajectory by varying weight distribution at impact; if I wanted to make a high shot, I'd just keep some of my weight back. It was like a teeter-totter. High shot, weight back. Low shot, weight forward, thereby altering the loft on the club at impact.
It had also become apparent that the curvature of the ball depends on the plane relative to the target. As long as I was swinging toward my target, then the idea was to alter the plane to change curvature. And I could change the plane simply by drawing the right foot back for a right-to-left shot, or by moving it forward for a left-to-right shot. It was simply a matter of altering alignment.

I'd also realized an important factor concerning Hogan's placement of his left foot. He wasn't doing this only to establish a balance point so that he could finish flat on his foot. He did it to set up a point at which his swing would stop when he was facing the target. That gave him a place to go to and the direction for the ball. It set up a resistance in the left knee and hip that would stop him directly on the target. This was a superb way of ensuring direction.
When I went out in 1961, then, I was feeling pretty good. That year I won the Coral Gables Open. I was swinging pretty well, but I still needed another piece. That turned out to be extension, which I thought about quite a bit in the early 1960s. My arc was pretty much what it needed to be already because of my weight transfer, but I was still controlling the club, almost placing it at the top. It took a while to let go, to simply let the club track on its own once I'd started the swing. Eventually I got very relaxed and started getting the feeling of centrifugal force; I felt as if I were just

being carried along by the momentum of the clubhead tracking. That was the final piece. By 1964, I had become what people called a natural golfer. I felt powerful while relaxed; it seemed as if centrifugal force were pulling my arms out of my shoulder sockets. That's when the game started to exhilarate me.

And yet there were problems. I still really couldn't explain what I was doing to my satisfaction, not totally anyway. I still believed I had to maneuver myself and the golf club. I'd learned all these parts of the swing that added up to what looked like a natural golfer, but I didn't really feel like one. I may have had what observers felt was close to a perfect swing, but I had an imperfect understanding of myself. I still didn't appreciate, for example, that everything I had developed was based on balance. The grip is based on balance. Weight transfer is based on balance. The finishing position is based on balance. Balance is the most important aspect of the swing. Had I been able to tell somebody then what I was doing, it would have been that I was keeping the swing in balance. But I was doing it by trial and error. I may have *made* myself into a natural golfer, but I hadn't let go of the mechanics.

I was never as relaxed as I would have liked. My swing might not have had any disturbances, but I had plenty within myself. For one thing, I thought that I had to be physically strong to play golf the way I wanted to. I felt I needed physical endurance to handle the lifestyle and the strains of competing and being in contention. Strength would solve everything, or so I thought. And why not? If the tour was so rigorous, it made sense to beat it with raw power. Meanwhile, I had little or no idea that it would have been far better to simply relax. It wasn't natural for me to make myself into a bullfighter out there. But I tried. I repressed all my feelings and camouflaged them with brute force.

It didn't work. Eventually, I realized I needed mental, emotional, and physical balance. I had the mental balance since I understood the swing. But because I had put the swing together in pieces, without realizing that balance was the heart of it all, and that the various pieces were nothing more than connective tissue that tied the starting position to the finishing position, I couldn't relax. So I had very little emotional balance and only rarely experienced physical pleasure.

A good example of how I lacked awareness was what happened to me after the 1966 World Cup in Tokyo. That's when I hit what I call my perfect shot, in the third round.

The aesthetics felt right to me. I was playing from a valley to an elevated green, and the air was so clear that I could visualize exactly what I wanted to do. I had no difficulty at all in selecting the type of shot I wanted to play. I was also in the heat of battle, in a very concentrated state.

I executed the shot and had this total mental, emotional, and physical experience. The shot came off to sheer perfection. The ball zipped by the hole, 180 yards away and uphill, and finished just a few feet away. I still don't know how it didn't go in. I don't know whether I'd even dreamed I could play a shot that well. It was a feeling of, "Hey, I can't do it any better. Is *that* any good? Give me more of that."

I came home wanting more of this experience. I went directly to the range at Oakdale to see if I could get it. I practised and I practised but I couldn't get the same response. Finally, I stopped and said, "You fool, you have to be in the heat of battle. You can't get it while you're practising." I needed total involvement.

WINNING PHOENIX
AND TUCSON

In 1968, I won the Phoenix and Tucson Opens in consecutive weeks. I played so well those two weeks, but really no better than in five other events I had played early that year. I really don't think I could have made better golf swings than during those seven weeks. The fact is that I could have won five out of the seven tournaments if I'd made some putts. That's how well I was playing. My swing was as good as it has ever been. At Phoenix and Tucson, I hit the ball so close to the hole that I couldn't miss.

And yet something was missing in the overall picture. I just wasn't feeling right. Something was out of balance.

Since October of 1966, I'd worked on a fitness programme in Toronto with the late Lloyd Percival. I'd found that I couldn't play more than a couple of weeks in a row without becoming physically and emotionally depleted. I was getting totally exhausted: no starch left at all after one competitive week.

The next week would be a washout. At 135 pounds, I had neither the durability nor the strength to play the way I was capable of. I thought I needed a programme that would give me more endurance.

By the time that 1968 season had begun, I was up to 172 pounds. I'd worked out with weights. I'd done isometrics and running. Now I felt I could keep going. I didn't get drained nearly as easily. This was important to me. I'd won four tour events by the beginning of the 1968 season, but I hadn't proven to myself that I could contend week after week. But in 1968, I played the first seven tournaments of the season, and, as I've said, contended every week. I was stronger. I wanted to see what I could do.

I started my first round in Phoenix on the back nine. I felt like I couldn't miss a shot.

That's what I'd been after all those years: the security of knowing where the ball would go. On my thirteenth hole, the fourth, I hit a shot eight feet left of the flag and twelve feet short. Not too bad by ordinary standards. But I was playing so well that Dave Marr, with whom I was playing, asked, "Where did that come from?" It seemed like a horrible shot. That's how high a player's standards can get when he knows where the ball is going. And I knew. I was absolutely knocking the flag down, stuffing it down the throat every hole. The game was very easy, and it stayed easy. Even though I didn't get much sleep the night before the last round – I had a one-shot lead, and would rather have been a shot or two behind – I still had enough strength to go on and win. That was gratifying. My endurance programme seemed to be paying off.

Tucson was even better. I was four strokes from the lead heading into the last round and figured a 66 would get me into a playoff. I told my caddy as we went to the tenth tee that 32 on the back side would do it. Then I shot 31 and won outright. Again, I was feeling powerful. My play down the stretch showed it.

On the seventeenth, I hit a shot within a foot of the hole. On the eighteenth, a 465-yard four-par, I hit driver, six-iron. The other guys were coming in with four-woods and long irons. I must have carried that last drive 280 yards, and the hole is a dynamic driving hole: water left and right with a camelback fairway. Miss the ball just a bit and it's in the water. But I nailed the drive, knocked the iron on the green, two-putted, and won.

You'd think I would have been ecstatic. After all, I had just won two in a row. I should have been elated. But instead, I was exhausted. I'd again been pushed to my emotional and physical limit. Sure, I'd gone longer this time. But inside I was hurting. I felt I was going to explode. The fact was that I had turned myself into a physically strong being, but I was also controlling my emotional side to the point of total exhaustion. I knew what the swing was all about – I'd studied the thing for so long – but I still wasn't aware that I didn't have to contrive it. I still didn't know that I didn't need to forcibly control the club and myself. I was still quite a ways from realizing that if I could just set up to the ball properly, incorporate the fundamentals, feel relaxed, and let it all go, then I would have a great time at golf.

One example will demonstrate what I mean. In 1968, I still felt that I had to hold on tightly to the club. To me that meant I would be in control of the clubhead. Grip strength, grip strength, grip strength. I thought golf was a physical game, but it's not. Not the way I thought: you don't need to lift barbells. But I was into strength and control, what I call disciplines. I'd stressed the back of my hands so much as a kid while I was into Charles Atlas bodybuilding that I couldn't play in some tournaments then. Sure, it's good to be strong. It helps because then you don't need to tense up to hold the club. Snead once said that you want to hold the club as if you're holding a bird in your hand. Fine. He has such strong forearms and hands that he can do this. Grip strength is important in the sense that you then don't have to tense your body to hang on to the club.

But I didn't understand it this way then. I wanted the vise-like grip that I believed would ensure passive hands and a stable clubface. That was non-interference to me. It took a lot of letting go in my later years as a tour player, and while I was teaching, to realize that it's enough just to hold the club lightly, enough just to feel the skin of the grip against the hands. Now, I stand up to the ball and I feel as if I'm hardly holding on to the club. That's freedom. That's balance. Then, I just let the club go where it will. But in those days I didn't understand these things. I was still controlling. I was still holding on with my mind and my body. I didn't know how to relax, and that was sad. This is the fear of losing control. It comes from a lack of understanding.

I was a wreck after I got back from Arizona. The city of Toronto held a civic reception for me and I received messages of congratulations from all over Canada. The trouble was, all I was feeling was the need to let go of my stress. I'd incubated so much pressure in those seven weeks, I just wanted to hide; I couldn't handle all the demands on my time.

Then I missed the cut at Doral in Miami when I went back on tour. After that I played only sporadically the rest of the year. I'd learned a hard lesson at Doral: that I was incapable of relaxing. And I never played the tour in quite the same way again.

When I look back on those years, I see that I didn't need to turn myself into a machine. Had I understood that the natural swing happens to be the logical swing, I wouldn't have locked myself up or constrained myself. I could have set up in the proper starting form and then connected through weight transfer to a proper finishing form. I would have understood that the swing didn't have to be so consuming. I couldn't let go in those days because I didn't know what would be there the next day if I did. While I was very sure of what worked for me, I didn't really understand it as a complete unified theory. I had built a machine and I thought it would break down if I didn't keep using it. The funny thing was that I knew all I needed to know about the golf swing, but I didn't know how to communicate it. Even in my own mind it was still a series of pieces. That's why golf consumed me. I was like the guy who goes to bed at night wondering if his swing will still be there in the morning.

After 1968, I still played the tour, but only part-time. I kept looking for something to replace the tour. That was tough. I stayed out there because I couldn't find a replacement. You can't spend all your life doing something and then just walk away from it. From 1972, after I won the Kaiser International Open in Napa, California while on my way to Japan with my wife, Shirley, I was strung out all the time, so used to agony I didn't know it.

The Kaiser had been the first time I'd felt joyful after winning. It was the first time I let go to any degree. I had been so locked into what I was doing prior to that. Shirley said it was so nice to see me smiling for having won rather than for just having performed well. It wasn't that I had given up being a perfectionist; it was that I had finally been able to enjoy the competition. I hadn't put so much pressure on myself that week.

But I had a terrible time with myself after the Kaiser. I had been used to winning by being intense. Suddenly, I was enjoying it. I had played with Jack Nicklaus the first two rounds, and he said that nobody was going to beat me. It was happening. I was at a natural state. However, I still had the dilemma of being in a place I didn't want to be in: I just didn't like the travelling.

Never again did I have the feeling I had in Napa. Maybe I was too immature to handle the lifestyle. But after my three sons reached school age, I couldn't stand being away from them.

And Shirley, of course, couldn't travel as much with me. I hated the isolation, but I kept at it. I should have left the tour then, but I didn't know what to do with myself.

LEARNING TO TEACH

Then in the late 1970s, I discovered teaching, which I've thoroughly enjoyed since. The day after I got home from Florida in 1978 was the day I started writing notes to myself about teaching. I wanted to communicate what I knew. But I had no teaching skills. It had been enough to learn for myself. But I couldn't sit down with people and tell them in acceptable fashion what I was experiencing. What had happened was that I wasn't questioning my emotions, the response I was getting from myself. And I only started putting it all together when others started questioning me. My experiences have made it possible for me to talk with people about their own tensions. But tension is unnecessary. Golf can be a pleasure.

Fortunately, I met a few people along the way who helped me see this. One fellow was Richard Lonetto, a sports psychologist at the University of Guelph. He had worked with other athletes on developing skills like balance and rhythm, and one day he took me out to Glen Abbey and had me play that round with my eyes closed. I was also hooked up to a heart monitor at the same time. That's the day I shot 67 with my eyes closed on full swings. My heartbeat was so slow that I might have been meditating. Lonetto showed me that I didn't need to see the ball as long as I had a pure form. Since that day I've done a lot of unsighted practice. It's amazing how quickly you can learn if you're in balance, and how much of a one-piece motion the swing really is. It's further proof that golf is not a hand-eye game. The ball just sits there. If you set up in a correct starting position and connect it to the finishing position while using laws of motion effectively, you'll contact the ball along the way.

This insight freed me. It really woke me up. I was amazed that I could make such a free swing without watching the ball. Here was a major clue: if we set up properly and simply made a motion to a target, then we didn't have to think about the ball. We would repeat the motion every time. The ball would simply get in the way.

Golfers have accepted so much. And they tend to accept that golf can't be natural. But you shouldn't mess with Mother Nature. Letting nature work frees us to enjoy golf. The game can be good for us if we allow things to happen. It's an entirely different experience from trying to make them happen. Once we understand the mechanics of the natural swing motion, we can use the natural laws to our advantage. Then we can give up the controls. Then we can fly. Then we won't tie ourselves in knots every time we contemplate a golf shot.

Balance is the underpinning of the natural swing motion. It's the heart of my philosophy. I advocate a balanced, natural golf swing, one you can use for the rest of your life.

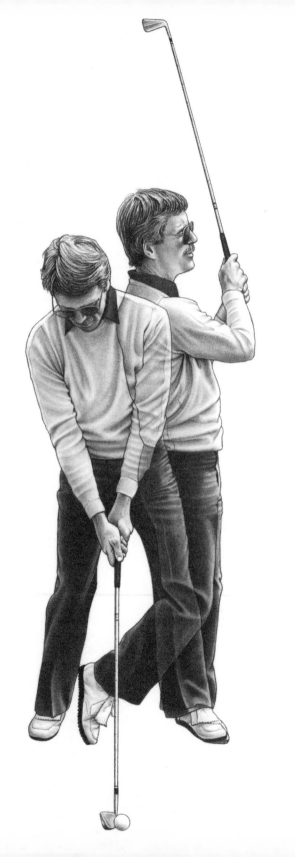

3. The Theory of the Natural Swing

MY CONTENTION is that golf is a target game. This means that the swing is a motion toward the target, not toward the ball. If it is a motion, it must conform to the laws of centrifugal force and inertia. We'll consider these in detail in a moment. Right now, I'd like to give you an overall impression of the motion. As you read the following description, try to visualize and sense the motion.

The golf swing motion is a means of connecting a starting position to a finishing position, everything being set up and performed in balance throughout. This is a natural happening based on a logical sequence of events deriving from physical laws of centrifugal force and inertia, performed under the governance of balance. We move the mass – the hands, arms, and club – by moving the body. Power is

transmitted through the body to the clubhead. The mass moves by weight transfer and rotation; we do nothing consciously with the hands, arms, and club. We assume a symmetrical starting form by distributing our weight evenly between the left foot and the right foot. We then transfer weight by moving to the right foot, while rotating around our trunk. We thereby control the motion by controlling the centre.

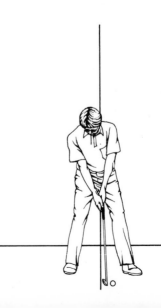

Footwork carries the club.

The swing motion is a transfer of weight performed in conjunction with a body turn. (We will discuss the motion in terms of the right-handed golfer.) Having completed the backswing, or what I call the loading motion, we then transfer weight by moving to our left foot – as we do while walking – to begin the downswing, or unloading motion.

When we complete the loading motion, seventy-five per cent of our weight will be on our right foot. At the end of the motion, one hundred per cent of our weight will be on our left foot.

All of our weight does not go to our right foot during the loading motion because the head, moving freely as we make no effort to keep it still, more or less faces the ball. During the unloading motion, though, the transfer of weight to the left foot and the move through the ball toward the target allows the head to face the target at the finish. We finish solidly on our left foot at natural height, with knees, hips, and shoulders facing the target and in immaculate balance.

It is important to emphasize that we do nothing consciously with the hands, wrists, and arms during the motion. They merely extend symmetrically from the centre and move due to the body motion. Footwork carries the body. This promotes clubhead security and guarantees a constant blade angle throughout the swing. There's no need to manipulate the clubhead. Proper footwork promotes a constant blade angle.

A proper starting form and a proper finishing form allow the momentum of the mass – the arms, hands, and golf club – to flow as it will during the swing. We pre-set in the starting form the circumstances that will enable us to make an uninterrupted motion toward a target. We take care of as much as possible by assuming a proper starting form. We want to give ourselves the best chance of making a pure motion.

If you start in a good position and you finish in a good position, not much can go wrong in between. That's the beauty of the natural, relaxed golf swing that incorporates the laws of motion. That's the beauty of balance.

The swing is one continuous motion.

THE LAWS OF MOTION IN THE GOLF SWING

The golf swing is governed by a set of physical laws familiar to anybody who has studied Grade Eleven physics. What do these laws say and how are they applicable to the swing motion?

Centrifugal Force

In its simplest terms, centrifugal force is the outward force acting on a body that is rotating in a circle around a central point. The central point in the swing motion is the trunk of a golfer's body, specifically a point right around his navel. The golf club rotates around this central point as we move our weight from the centre to the right foot, or first pivot point in the motion, and on to the left foot, or second pivot point.

Centrifugal force is powerful. It pulls the golf club outward

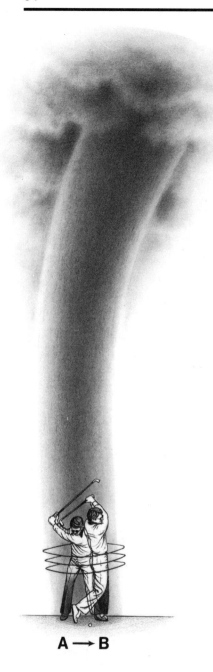

A → B

The power of centrifugal force as we move from loading to unloading.

and downward as the player moves toward the target. It can generate clubhead speeds of more than one hundred m.p.h. and gives the player a feeling of tremendous energy. Moreover, the wider the arc of the swing, the more power generated, and, ultimately, the greater the distance the ball will travel.

Centrifugal force generates a feeling of our arms being pulled out of their sockets. We control the periphery, that is, the club, by controlling the centre. We put the clubhead in delay when we unload or transfer weight to the left foot. And all we are doing is transferring weight and rotating around a central point. The inside, to be sure, isn't moving that much. It's like the eye at the centre of a storm, the centre force that creates a tornado. The inner controls the outer. It's much easier and much more efficient to control the clubhead from the centre than to try to do so by manipulating it – as I did when I first hit balls on the range at St. Charles.

Inertia

This law of physics states that an object, once set into motion, will continue in its state of uniform motion unless otherwise disturbed by an outside force.

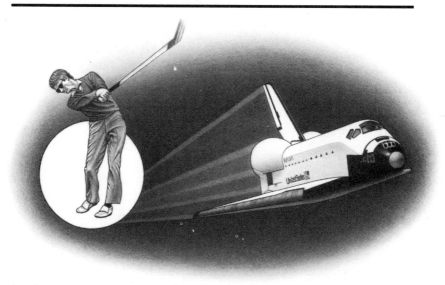

Inertia.

The reader may ask: what does this principle have to do with the golf swing?

Applied to the golf swing, this law implies that if we set the clubhead in motion, it will tend to remain along the path of that motion unless we interfere. For example, if we set up with the clubface facing the target, or square to the target line, the blade angle will remain constant unless we *deliberately* disturb its original angle. (We can disturb the angle by twisting our hands or lifting them or maneuvring them in any number of ways which change the angle – that is, alter the angle and path of the clubhead.) It stands to reason, then, that we do nothing consciously with the arms, wrists, and hands during the swing so as not to disturb the intended path.

If centrifugal force is the governing factor in generating power in the swing, then inertia is the governing factor in producing consistency. How is this so? Consistency occurs when the

Rotation of trunk of the body.

golfer is able to *repeat* his swing by letting it travel along the same path every time. We repeat the swing motion by doing nothing to interfere with the path of the clubhead; that is, we allow the law of inertia to keep the blade angle constant.

Bearing in mind these two laws of physics, let us examine how they operate in executing the swing motion.

The Swing Motion

The swing motion is a means of connecting a starting position to a finishing position. The key word is *connecting*. This connection can be achieved naturally during the motion – that is, by allowing the laws of motion to prevail. Let's run through the sequence of the swing motion and identify where each law of motion comes into play.

You prepare for the swing motion by setting up a starting form in which you are in balance. Your weight is equally distributed between both feet. You then transfer weight to your right foot while rotating the club around the trunk of your body. I like to refer to this stage of the motion as ''loading''; you load up on power, or generate potential energy.

The loading motion requires two elements: 1) that the arc (that is, the measure of the outer circumference of the circle on which the clubhead travels) is maximized so that centrifugal force can work its magic in generating power; and 2) that your hands and arms do not interfere with the natural rotation of the loading, or, as it's commonly known, the backswing motion. In other words, once we start the loading motion we do nothing to interfere with the natural path the club will take. We allow inertia to work.

Why do we transfer weight and rotate during the loading motion as opposed to, for example, picking the club up and swinging it along a path? The answer, clearly, is that weight transfer is the most effective means of moving the clubhead so that we can create inertia *in* the clubhead. We don't want to consciously use our hands, arms, or shoulders since this destroys the integrity of the motion. And so we transfer weight. This removes any conscious hand action from the motion.

Take a club in your hands now and assume a starting form. Don't concern yourself with what you look like. Now, simply hold on to the club and let your weight shift back toward your right foot. Notice how far the clubhead has travelled, *without you doing anything consciously with your hands, arms, or shoulders*. You initiated the motion through

footwork and the clubhead went along. You let inertia work. Footwork and weight transfer are the most effective means of making a motion.

The swing motion is also a rotary motion if we are to do it in balance. As we transfer weight back, we allow our hands, arms, and clubhead to rotate around our trunk while transferring weight to our right foot. (If we didn't do so, we would soon roll to the outside of our right foot and lose balance.) The club continues to track on its own due to inertia; as the centrifugal force starts to supply its power, the clubhead continues to move back, uninterrupted.

The "unloading" motion, or downswing, involves a weight shift toward the target so that at the end of the swing one

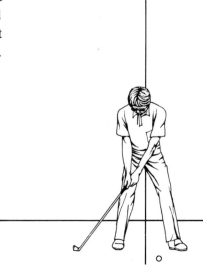

hundred per cent of our weight is on our left foot. As in the loading motion, we must maximize our arc in order to achieve maximum power and minimize any interference with the clubhead path so as to maintain control. By doing so we achieve both power and control.

The Importance Of Balance

We will create consistency and power only if we maintain balance throughout the entire motion. Without proper balance, centrifugal force and therefore clubhead speed are compromised. Without balance, our hands, arms, or shoulders can interfere with the motion, forcing us to sacrifice consistency.

Balance governs the swing motion. The better balanced we are, the better our chances of producing a fluid swing motion. The best swing gives direction and power in balance.

The essence of the natural golf swing, then, entails connecting a starting position to a finishing position. The connection is best achieved through weight transfer and rotation. In the backswing, we "load" up with power by shifting weight to the right foot. In the down-

swing, we "unload" the power by transferring all the weight to the left foot. The angle at which we set our left foot in the starting form – and it is slightly different for every golfer depending on flexibility – creates a point of resistance in the left knee and hip so that our bodies stop directly on the target. This is the source of direction. It's a pointer; we're going to get there.

During the course of the weight transfer and rotation, the basic laws of motion apply in generating maximum power and control, neither of which can be fully realized without good balance. Seen as a motion, the swing is not complicated. There's no need to break it down into 1,001 components. The means of understanding the swing as a sequence of movements that happen naturally once we initiate the motion are available. My goal is to present you with an overall, comprehensive theory that will take care of what I call the "by-the-way" or "involuntary" happenings that occur during the motion. You won't need to concern yourself with the minutiae that lead to paralysis by analysis. You'll learn to evaluate every one of your swings according to just a few factors,

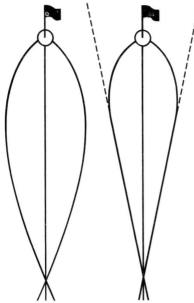

Curvature due to alignment relative to target.

Power is a function of a maximum arc combined with weight transfer – the arc being the distance the club travels while we are in balance, or the perimeter of the plane. Centrifugal force is the main source of power; its effect multiplies when combined with weight transfer.

Inertia and centrifugal force work together to allow the golfer to produce a controlled, consistent, and powerful motion. If we set up in a balanced position and maintain a balanced route by not interfering with what we have, the motion will repeat every time. We're giving up control to gain control. We're letting physics take over. We're marrying the principles of the swing motion to principles of the physical being.

and you'll be able to understand these factors both intellectually and physically, given the theory and the drills.

To review: the most effective swing is one which produces consistency and power in balance.

Consistency depends on a pure plane, the path the clubhead travels relative to a target. Inertia is the primary source of consistency. A pure plane will produce curvature, that is, straight, left-to-right, or right-to-left shots. We design curvature into the shot by assuming a starting alignment relative to a target.

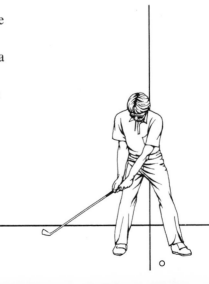

4. Balance: The Most Important Fundamental

M ORE THAN any other quality that they have in common, athletic champions are "in balance." It's a wonderful quality to observe, this ability to remain stabilized while in motion. It's nothing less than *the* identifying characteristic of elite athletes, whether the performer is baseball batter Don Mattingly, sprinter Ben Johnson, hockey genius Wayne Gretzky, or golfer Seve Ballesteros. Their grace of form and ease of movement make us take notice. To me, these athletes are displaying something beautiful. The majesty of his golfing form drew me to Ben Hogan, and the same thing today draws me to Ballesteros. There is a harmony in their movements, a quietness or stillness. They are centered. From that centre they generate swing motions that in my opinion rival in simplicity and connection of sequences the most inspiring of dances. I don't think it's an exaggeration to consider the swing motion a dance. Mikhail Baryshnikov moves elegantly and powerfully in space; he thrills us because he is so exquisitely balanced and can thus probe the edges of the space in which he is dancing. So can the well-balanced golfer. He can push himself to the limit because he is aware of the edge that he cannot go beyond without losing balance.

The golfer who can sense his swing as a dance will be able to change his focus. Instead of seeing the ball and a hit, he will focus on his body and a swing; here is where he can most productively place his attention. Imagine yourself as this golfer, moving back and forth with a golf club in your hands. Feel yourself exploring the range of movement permissible for you – given your physique and flexibility – without losing balance.

MENTAL, EMOTIONAL, AND PHYSICAL BALANCE

By balance I don't mean only the kind of stability we associate with movement. The kind of balance you need to develop the natural golf swing is a balance of mind, body, and emotion. A swing theory that is based on balance must incorporate this more comprehensive idea, and show that it is impossible to make a coherent swing motion while out of balance in any area.

The kind of balance I advocate begins with a logical conception of the swing. The golfer who knows what he is trying to do will have mental balance.

He will stand up to every shot confident that his method makes sense. He will approach each shot with the certainty that if he carries out his procedures properly he cannot help but produce a good swing. But he must know what he is trying to do. Given that, he can accept error. He is, after all, a human being. This is why I say that it isn't so much what we do as what we attempt to do that counts. We will make mistakes. We will revert to old habits. But we can progress as long as we understand what we are trying to do.

Such knowledge promotes emotional balance. The golfer who has a clear conception of the swing motion will be able to ward off the insults the game brings. The golfer who has procedures to follow won't be buffeted by emotion. A routine will give him something to do; he will take care of time, one of golf's major challenges. There is too much time for us to think in golf; and if we don't know what to think about, we'll probably worry. The game will beat us if we are prone to such anxiety. The golfer who follows his procedures with each shot, however, will be in a concentrated state. He has something to do on each shot, and that gives him the best chance for making a correct motion.

The knowledgeable golfer will also be impervious to the confusion and anxiety that poor shots can cause. Anxiety is due to a lack of awareness. Most golfers don't know why they hit a good or bad shot. They wonder why such and such happened. They play without a foundation from one swing to the next and judge their play solely by the result they get. It doesn't matter to them if the ball has flown in the opposite direction to the one intended; they're content as long as the ball finishes in play or on the green. If they get a good result, they think they made a decent swing. Well, maybe they did. But what chance have they of repeating the swing if they don't know what causes what? Where's their security?

The golfer who understands the concept of the natural golf swing won't feel anxious. He will be able to evaluate every swing to see where he went wrong, and go on to the next one. He will be trying to do the same thing with each swing motion. This is because he understands the factors behind the basic swing. Evaluation and assessment enable him to consider the causes of his misplays, and then forget them. This will encourage emotional balance. He will gradually learn to play one shot at a time and by doing so will be able to enjoy the game more. This happens when we take the pressure off any one shot. Knowledge breeds confidence and calmness. The relaxed golfer can play the game and accept its ups-and-downs while the agitated golfer may find himself terrified of the next challenge.

The concentrated state that I am describing isn't easily come by. We need to be vigilant so that we might modify our behaviour and ensure we do not play a shot while feeling disorganized. The slightest feeling of

discomfort over the ball must be enough to warn us away from the impending stroke.

Who can forget, to cite one example, the four-iron that Seve Ballesteros struck into the water in front of the fifteenth green during the 1986 Masters? The shot was a weak, pulled effort and effectively cost him the Masters, notwithstanding Jack Nicklaus's brilliant rush of seven-under-par golf over the last ten holes to take the tournament. Ballesteros was in position to hit the green and perhaps eagle the hole. Instead, he lost concentration and misplayed the shot.

Later, Ballesteros said that he was indecisive over the ball, that he ought to have played a hard five-iron since he was feeling so charged up. But he didn't monitor his emotional state at the moment. He let anxiety get the better of him instead of stepping away from the ball to better assess how he was feeling.

I had a similar experience during the last round of the 1966 Masters in Augusta, Georgia while in contention and on the twelfth tee. Eager to learn my exact position and possibilities, I had a look at the scoreboard behind the eleventh green. That in itself wasn't a good idea, as it took my mind off my plan of playing one shot at a time. Anyway, I looked, and figured if I could birdie the par-five thirteenth and fifteenth holes along with one other, I might get into a playoff. Filled with anticipation and nearly detonating with adrenalin, I could hardly get my feet on the ground as I teed it up on the twelfth, that gorgeous and tricky par-three where Rae's Creek sits in front of the green.

What was I going to do? I was so excited that I couldn't settle down. But I had to play the shot. I thought, well, I'll just hit the ball between the bounces of my feet. So I took the six-iron and hit the ball just on the front edge of the green – from where it spun back into the creek. Now I had to drop and take a shot penalty, but I did get up-and-down from the tee side of the creek for bogey. The adrenalin burst lasted just that one swing on the tee, but it was enough. It cost me any chance of getting into a playoff.

Later, I assessed what had happened. I'd gotten ahead of myself, out of balance. Anticipation got the better of me. I'd given in to it. Then I saw Arnold Palmer. He'd won the tournament in 1958, 1960, 1962, and 1964. I related the story of what had happened to me on the twelfth tee.

Palmer said, ''So what's new about that? I was like that the entire last round in 1958.'' The difference was that Palmer was able to play through it. I didn't know what to do with the feelings. I should have calmed myself down after looking at the scoreboard. But I didn't realize how important it was to be emotionally balanced. I wasn't aware of how closely I had to monitor myself.

Not long ago, I had another illuminating experience while I was out hitting balls. I'd made a few nice passes with a five-iron, after which I started swinging a three-iron. Ten or twelve swings into my practice session, I noticed that I wasn't feeling as free-wheeling through the ball as I normally do. Stepping back,

I stopped for a moment and chuckled. As much as I know how important it is to evaluate each swing according to whether or not I was in balance – and a few other fundamentals I will teach you – I hadn't been doing so. I'd fallen into driving range boredom: hitting one shot after another without setting up properly, without thinking about what I was trying to do. No wonder I'd lost the sense of freedom. Here was a useful object lesson. It suggested I had better keep my mind on what I was doing. Bad habits are a mere lapse of concentration away.

Now even when you understand that mental balance or knowledge leads to emotional balance, you must still keep an eye on your responses. It's self-

knowledge. You have to learn what emotions work for you. Do you need quiet or excitement? Do you like to chit-chat while you're playing or would you rather play golf as if it were chess, silently? Are you a fast walker or do you prefer a modest pace?

Palmer likes the excitement. Fellows such as Julius Boros, Gene Littler, or Larry Nelson prefer something milder. Ballesteros seems to want to conquer, and needs the right venue to get in the conquistador spirit. He was exhilarating when he won the 1984 British Open over the Old Course at St. Andrews, Scotland, and equally thrilling when he led the British-European team to its first Ryder Cup victory on American soil in the fall of 1987. Perhaps this is why he seems to court controversy in the golf world. He needs to feel fired up. It's the dynamo in him.

Whatever your disposition, you will learn to lessen your anxiety as you come to understand the natural golf swing.

Lowering your anxiety will allow you to learn about yourself on the course. Anxiety impedes self-knowledge; it's all we can think about when we're beset by the feeling. Yet it's the emotional state in which most of us are locked.

You will, however, progress as you practise the natural golf swing and learn to evaluate both your poor swings and your successful ones. Mental and emotional balance will open you up to the physical pleasures that come with a coordinated swing motion. You will appreciate that the graceful swing is also the pleasurable swing. As you experience more enjoyment from the motion itself, you will more easily drop your old habits and ways of thinking.

PRE-GAME BALANCE

I've always thought that preparation is one of the most important aspects of golf. We want to set up an environment in which we have the best chance of performing to the maximum of our ability. I like to stack the deck, but it's still too easy to go to the course with the wrong cards. It's happened to me plenty of times.

Consider the ways in which we can get out of balance even before we pick up a club. For one thing, we may set up imbalances in the way we approach the game. Imagine the following situation, one that I'm sure we're all familiar with.

You've got a game arranged for eleven o'clock. You've known about it for two weeks. Somehow, though, you've neglected to organize your morning schedule so that you can arrive at the course in plenty of time for your game. Come 10:30, you scream out of your office and tear along the highway to the course. You're pulling off your tie as you drive into the parking lot, and putting on your shoes with five minutes to go before your tee-time. Of course, you haven't given a moment's thought to your strategy for the first tee. You jog out there nearly out of breath, say hello to your friends as you grab the driver from your bag, stick a tee in the ground, and whack your first shot out of bounds.

Foolish start, wouldn't you agree? But we're all guilty of it. And yet when we hit our opening shot poorly, we still tend to blame our swings. Sure, the swing was the culprit, but it's only a reflection of the imbalances we allowed ourselves to feel beforehand. The swing reflects what was going on in our nervous system. Errors in the swing often begin with errors in the mind.

Balance means *setting up an environment in which you can do your best work.* This comes from knowledge, application, and preparation. The golfer who doesn't have a clear idea of what he is trying to do will be one scared golfer. He'll be jerky and out-of-sorts.

In the mid-sixties, I was playing an exhibition not far from Vancouver. We were flying into Seattle in a little amphibious plane when we ran into trouble. It looked like the thing would go under, but somehow we got

to the dock. I got my stuff together, raced to the car, and made it to the course just in time. The starter was giving me last call to the tee. And what did I do? Exactly what you might think. I knocked the ball out of bounds.

That's not the way to balance. Preparation *is*. I normally get up three hours in advance of my tee time and do everything in a nice leisurely way. When I played the U.S. tour, I'd even drive to the course at fifty miles an hour in a sixty-miles-per-hour zone. Never would I exceed the speed limit. Along the way I'd think about how the course might play that day, the shots I'd need. Then I'd go to the range and play every shot I could anticipate. It didn't matter what club I had in my hands because I was working with the swing motion. It wasn't that I hit a driver on the range and then a four-iron, as if I were playing the first hole. My mind was on the swing itself, and so I could work with a wedge or a driver. The point was that I was working creatively, not just banging balls. I had a purpose.

By the time I got to the first tee, then, I'd reviewed the course on my way to the club, and then played it in my mind while on the range. I was giving myself a chance by preparing properly. I didn't want to self-destruct because of poor preparation. It was all in the interest of balance.

I can hear you say to yourself: "This is all very well for Knudson, this business of getting up three hours before his tee-off time to prepare for his round. He plays the game for a living. But I don't. I've got things to do at home and the office. I can't take that much time. I'm lucky to get to the course in time to have a coffee, never mind a leisurely warm-up session."

Fair enough. I appreciate that you may not have the time I do. But I make the point anyway. I don't want you to do anything at the expense of balance. Maybe you shouldn't plan a golf game if you know you don't have the time to prepare properly. Better to take care of business, then practise a while and play nine holes. Why exasperate yourself? Do it right and you'll be further ahead in the long run.

You don't play golf, you see, to relax. You relax to play golf. I don't think you'll find a balanced, relaxed state on the course if you haven't brought it with you. You may still want to play, but don't be surprised if you can't perform as well as you'd like. Don't be too hard on yourself. Assess your mental and emotional state. It's easy but disastrous to be in one place physically and in another mentally.

Assessment is part of being balanced. You can't always be one hundred per cent involved, but at least by assessing the situation you won't take the results too seriously. You'll know where they're coming from. You can only rectify a problem if you are aware of what it is.

BALANCE IN THE SWING

You now know that the golf swing at its most basic is a means of connecting a proper starting position to a proper finishing position through weight transfer and rotation. Now we will develop a form governed by balance. For example, I want to find a way to avoid *forcing* myself to do anything in the swing. I don't want to *make* my left arm stay straight. I don't want to lock my head in a rigid

position. I don't want to grip the club tightly or stoop to the ball. These positions ruin balance. The golfer who is in balance is one who is doing things naturally. He's not trying so hard. The observer sees freedom rather than tightness, smoothness rather than effort.

There *are* positions that we achieve during the swing, that *are* very much a part of the efficient swing motion. But I don't want to *make* these happen; I want to *let* them happen. I want to find a form that will connect the starting position to the finishing position in such a way that all the good things occur naturally. I want to find a form in which I can just start the swing in motion and let it go on its own. I want to find a form that

will generate a path for the club-head that will repeat every time, and in which I don't have to interfere. And I want to do so in balance.

Two forms of balance are important in the conception of the natural swing motion itself: they are static and dynamic balance.

STATIC BALANCE

We are in static balance when we are centered and still and when we have assumed a coordinated, natural position. The golfer who is well-balanced in his starting position and at his finishing position is in static balance. If the golf swing is indeed a matter of connecting a starting position to a finishing position, then it is clear that we want to begin in balance and end in balance.

The golfer who develops an awareness of static balance will be able to find his centre. He will sense when his weight is evenly distributed between his feet during the starting position and will not begin the motion if he senses otherwise. He will know when he has assumed a

proper posture and grip, and when he is properly aligned to his target. He will *feel* whether or not he is in balance because he will have learned to become sensitive to what it means.

The same holds true for his finishing position, where one hundred per cent of his weight will be concentrated on his forward foot. If it is not, well, he will be out of balance at the end of his swing. He will not have swung through to his target. You will learn to evaluate these positions, and thereby become sensitized to the degree of balance during your starting and finishing positions. Your self-awareness will increase and along with it your ability to remain in balance will grow.

Static balance, then, is achieved by: (a) proper posture; (b) proper weight distribution; (c) proper grip; and (d) correct alignment to target.

DYNAMIC BALANCE

By dynamic balance I mean the quality of stability that is noticeable in first-class golfers while they are moving. They are centered while in motion. They glide through the sequence of movements that comprise the swing motion. They appear effortless, but only because they are working so efficiently. One aspect of the motion flows smoothly into the next.

You achieve dynamic balance by first putting yourself in static balance. You then allow inertia and centrifugal force to take over while transferring weight and rotating. By doing nothing to interfere with the motion, you ensure that you will be balanced while moving.

Contrast the dynamically balanced golfer with the one who scatters his energy all over the place with seemingly random movements. The former is connected from start to finish; the latter allows his arms to fly off into space while his legs remain stuck to the ground as if they're secured there with a ball and chain. There's no unity. The general impression is one of chaos. No wonder the unbalanced golfer whips his hands so abruptly into the ball; he doesn't know where he is in space; he is, of course, all over the place, and reacts by trying to get his club on the ball any way he can. It's all very inefficient, and unpleasant to watch. He's working too hard.

Think of yourself as a golfer who knows what it means to be in balance. You wouldn't tilt while walking down a level path, would you? Dynamic balance simply refers to that state you're in while moving with purpose and organization. It doesn't make sense to do otherwise.

Dynamic balance, then, is achieved by (a) incorporating all the elements in static balance (for if we are not balanced while we are not moving, we cannot be balanced while in motion); plus, (b) allowing for inertia to prevail; (c) passive hands; and (d) proper weight transfer.

5. The Starting Form

A FLAWLESS starting form gives us the best opportunity of making a proper swing motion. We set up in balance because we want to swing in balance. A balanced starting form gives us that chance. When we connect it to a balanced finishing form we ensure the desired result.

A balanced starting form accomplishes many good things. It sets the tone for the motion, for one, while promoting feelings of simplicity and freedom.

The starting form is totally within our control. We've gone a long way toward ensuring a positive result if we get it right.

Before we get into the components of the starting form, I'd like you to look at the illustration of the starting form that begins this chapter. The impression is of a golfer who is relaxed yet alert, at ease yet full of vitality. There's a feeling of being ready, in a "go" position. I have an impression of strength when I see golfers who are set up like this. They resemble boxers, or tae-kwon-do experts. They're prepared, ready to move. It seems that you couldn't budge them, they're so stable, but that

at the same time they're like cats, ready to spring loose. You can sense the energy coursing through their bodies.

By contrast, a golfer who is slumped over appears weak and sluggish. You could easily push him over. His body language speaks of withdrawal; he's given up before he starts. There's no feeling of intent, no sense of power. He's as sluggish as the other fellow is alive.

Keep the accompanying illustration in mind as you study the starting form. We're setting you up to make an aggressive move, an athletic move, one full of purpose and direction.

Let's look at the starting position in detail. We'll break it up into its components: target awareness, grip, stance in relation to target, alignment in relation to target, ball location relative to the body, and posture.

TARGET AWARENESS

Imagine that you are about to
play a standard shot with a five-
iron. You're not trying to curve
it any particular way; your goal
is a straight shot. Before you do
anything else, before you think
about grip or the other elements
in the starting position, get a
picture in your mind of the target. Imagine yourself swinging
through the ball toward the target
and beyond it, as I did while
swinging to the flagpole at St.
Charles. Feel yourself moving
back and forth. Let the image of
the motion that you will make
as you swing through the ball on
the way to the target fill your
mind's eye. Let it sink in, as if
it were a picture you were proj-
ecting onto a blank white wall.

The idea here is to plant the
image of the target in your mind.
It's the object to which you will
react. Golf in this way *is* a reaction game. It's not a hand-eye
game in which we react to a ball,
as I've emphasized, but a location game in which we react to a
target. The more vividly we can
imagine the target, the more
intensely will we react to it. You
can build up your powers of
target awareness at home by
closing your eyes and taking
yourself through your course,
shot by shot.

Having a clear image of the
target in your mind gets you
going. It gives you purpose, direction, and intent. How are
you going to get somewhere if
you don't know where you're
going? How are you going to
establish a route or a path to get
somewhere if you haven't decided upon your destination? The
more clearly you can fix your
destination in your mind, the
more easily will you reach your
objective. Target awareness
takes your mind's eye off the
ball and puts it where it belongs:
out there in space. That's real
direction. That's a goal. It helps
fix in your mind's eye the distance, direction, trajectory, and
curvature you're after with each
shot.

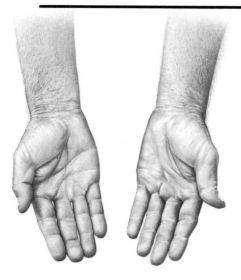

Start with hands compact; notice position of thumbs.

Hands opposed.

GRIP

Focused as you are on your target, you are also aware of balance. You want to adopt a grip that enables you to get your hands on the club in a balanced position. It stands to reason that the balanced grip is the one that most approximates the way in which your hands fall naturally. This means that you won't have to contort your hands in any way. Think of Roberto De Vicenzo, Peter Thomson, Sam Snead, Ben Hogan, Gene Littler, and Curtis Strange. These golfers get their hands on the club properly. Their hands look as if they belong on the golf club.

The natural grip is no different than a grip we would use for many tasks. It's also the one that sets us up so that we are oriented toward our target, if, that is, we have kept our focus on the target. The back of the left hand, or the left wrist, faces the target. This makes sense, since we want to contact the ball with our clubface square to the target; that is, at an angle of ninety degrees to the target. We form the grip so that the palms are opposed, as in prayer. Why do it differently? To grip the club with the left wrist pointing to the sky, for example, would force us to compensate somewhere during the motion. But we are designing a starting position that will allow us to make a simple, natural motion; without compensatory moves and extraneous gestures. We're designing a no-frills motion, so we start with a no-frills grip. Form follows function. Less is more.

The right hand opposes the left, as is evident in the illustrations. Put your arms in front of you with the fingers extended outward. Now put them palm to palm. This, in essence, is the grip. The hands and palms oppose one another. They are in balance with respect to the target and each other. Drop your arms down as if you have a club in your hands and the same relationship holds.

The club, of course, intervenes between the hands. We now want to find the most straightforward means of holding the club while maintaining the relationship to the target. The hands and palms still oppose one another, as in prayer.

Left Hand Placement on the Club

Fit the club diagonally across the palm of your left hand. It's positioned so that when the last three fingers of the left hand wrap around the butt end of the club, the meaty part of the hand applies pressure as well as the fingers. This is a balanced, trim condition in which you can actually control the club with the last three fingers of your left hand. The fingers apply pressure from the bottom and the right side of the club, while the meaty part of the hand applies pressure from the top and the left side of the club. This symmetrical arrangement generates a sensation of control and power in the left hand. The grip pressure happens naturally when you assume the correct form. I don't want you to

Left hand placement.

you have it when you feel some pressure from the base of your thumb against the upper part of your forefinger where they meet. This promotes unity in the hand. It's another measure of control. It helps you feel solid and energetic.

The left hand placement also does something else that comes in handy, given the objectives of the swing motion. We are trying to allow the mass of our club and hands and arms to move on a pure path. We want to develop a motion in which we don't consciously do a thing with our hands. They just go along for the ride. And therefore we want to design a starting form so that we can let them do just that. That's why we place the left hand on the club as we do and that's why I suggest a natural grip pressure. It all helps in avoiding slippage during the motion.

actually *apply* any pressure. Applied pressure is extra pressure. You'll find you have all the pressure you require simply by adopting the form. The form *gives* you the pressure. You need not do anything to create it.

The left thumb, meanwhile, fits nicely on top of the shaft. The inward pressure that you have organized through the placement of your hand on the club will ensure that the top of your left forefinger will push against your thumb. You'll know

You will feel that your left-hand grip is primarily a palm grip. This is as it should be. Pressure is bearing in from both sides of the club to keep the club in the palm of your left hand. It fits there because it belongs there and gives you your best chance of swinging in balance while retaining clubhead control.

Cultivate the sensation of the left-hand grip. It's one you will want to monitor every time you take your starting position. And it's one that will make you feel like a golfer from the instant you assume the grip.

Right Hand Placement

The right hand fits over the left. The little finger fits in and overlaps the space between the index finger and forefinger of the left hand. This has proven to be the most effective means of promoting unity between the hands.

As with the left hand, when you assume the proper form you will find that the upper part of the right thumb lightly presses against the upper extending part of the forefinger. Keep the grip compact and balanced and you'll find that the right hand simply folds over the left, enabling the left thumb to fit into the pocket that is thereby formed. The right-hand grip, then, is mostly in the fingers. The middle three fingers have the most contact with the club.

The right hand acts as a counterbalancing force on the club. It presses toward the left hand as the left presses toward the right.

Setting the right hand on the club.

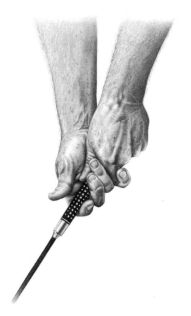

Setting the right hand on the club.   The completed grip.

The connection thus formed sets the tone for the starting form: hands united in strength and purpose. We have arranged the grip so that we need not consciously use our hands during the swing. The relationship of the hands and arms to the club will not change throughout the swing. We've put them on the club so that we can forget about them. This is the heart of clubhead control. If the hands are passive, the clubhead will also be passive.

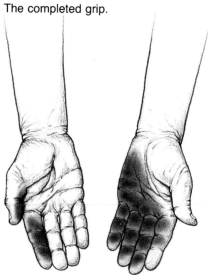

Pressure points.

STANCE

We've identified our target and gripped the club properly as part of assuming a balanced starting form. Now we want to get our feet right so that we'll be ready to make the motion.

We are considering a standard five-iron shot in which we visualize the ball flying straight and at normal trajectory and distance. We're doing this for the sake of convenience. It really doesn't matter what club we have in our hands, since the swing motion is the same for every club.

Given that we are planning a straight shot, there's no reason for us to align ourselves other than parallel left to the line of flight, give or take a few degrees. We set the right foot and clubface, then, at right angles to the target.

The left foot is in a slightly different position relative to the target. We set it at an angle of at least twenty-five degrees open to the target. I say "at least" because the degree of openness will vary for each golfer depending on his flexibility.

Why do we set the left foot open? For balance. We want to finish in balance, and so we must find a position for the left foot so that we will be standing on it at the finish. We practise positioning the left foot so that it sets up a resistance in the left knee and hip in order that our bodies are stopped directly on the target, facing it. The key is finding that location. I'll show you a drill later on that will help you find it. For now, stand with your left foot square, or at right angles to a target, and then open to the target. It's easy to see that you can move to your target more easily with the left foot open. This left foot placement will give you direction.

This might seem like an adjustment away from a natural starting position. It's not. If we're to make a motion toward the target, we must do so in balance. We won't be able to make the free motion if the left foot is square. We'll set up restrictions in the left hip and knee.

There's another factor to consider regarding left foot placement. This is the position of the foot relative to the left shoulder. You must place the left foot *outside* the left shoulder so that you will be able to finish with your weight on your left foot. Balance is the reason I advocate a wide stance; it allows you to finish flat on the left foot.

Most golfers roll toward the outside of the left foot. You're moving forward, though, and the best place for you to finish is solidly on the left foot, with one hundred per cent of your weight there, evenly distributed across the foot. This idea made so much sense to me after I saw Ben Hogan that I worked

and worked to achieve the position. Still, the habit of rolling over to the outside of my left foot was so ingrained that it took me a year and a half of practice until I could finish solidly on my left foot every time.

ALIGNMENT

Ideally, we want to set up square to the target. But we're not ideally built creatures, and so we must accept one important factor: every person has his own alignment that hits the ball straight, *for him*. It won't vary much from standard, but it will probably deviate just enough from geometric perfection to cause some concern among a person's friends. They'd rather he simulated a machine. But machines don't make golf swings. Human beings do, and we're all built differently.

I'm a good example. My right leg is five-eighths of an inch shorter than my left leg. That's why I set up slightly closed relative to my target. I've got to do this in order to stand level during the starting position and to give myself a chance to remain in balance during the motion. I want my weight distributed fifty-fifty between both my feet at address. If I set up square, too much of my weight would be on my right side because my right leg is shorter than my left. I therefore also have to keep my left leg flexed to maintain my balance. The adjustment I make to get in a balanced position is the same I make for playing from an uphill lie. I want to be level, to feel free. I'd do the same if I were ice-skating or skiing. I refuse to give in to a physical imbalance I was born with. That's why I adjust. It helps me arrive at a position from which I hit the ball straight. Sure, I'd like to stand square with my feet level, but I can't. I tried a lift in my right foot in the early 1960s, and it worked for a while. I could really make a move. It felt wonderful. But I had to give up the lift because it stressed my back muscles. So I made the adjustment.

You may not need to make as big an adjustment. I point mine out to you in the interests of the natural swing. It might also remind us of the primary factor in the natural swing: we don't do anything at the expense of balance.

The practice range is the place where we determine our personal alignment that allows us to hit the ball straight. This can change every day depending on how a person feels. I never get out of bed feeling the same from day to day. There's a physical variation in the human structure from day to day. Before we go to the course, then, we work on the range to establish the position from which we can hit the ball dead straight. That's square for that day. That's natural. We don't want to impose rules on the human frame. We adjust for the physical.

Having done so, we now consider our alignment to the target. The adjustment we made with the left foot to take the body to a finishing position has not only opened the foot relative to the target. It's also opened the knee and hip. Our shoulders are also open relative to the target because our right hand is lower on the club than our left.

Place your right hand under your left and you'll notice that your shoulders open. They have to. Yet we've been told to keep our shoulders square to the target. The usual advice is to stick our right elbow into our sides, thereby squaring up our shoulders. How many times have you seen a well-meaning golfer jam a club across his friend's right forearm and then try to shove it underneath his left elbow? This is supposed to be square. It might be geometrically square, but it isn't square for the purpose of the swing. It's an outrageous contortion that creates imbalance.

Alignment in relation to the target.

Square to the target is therefore somewhat to the left of the target. A line drawn through the heels would point either directly at the target, or a few degrees either way. A line drawn through the toes would point somewhat to the left of the target. This is the only naturally square position, even if it isn't mathematically precise. The important consideration is that each individual finds what is square for him, and plays from there. And square to the target for most golfers is open. Let's not fight it. Let's be in balance from the start.

To repeat: we make three adjustments in the starting form. We set the left foot open to the target for direction and balance; this opens our knees, hips, and shoulders relative to the target. (The shoulders are open also because when we grip the club the right hand is underneath the left.) At the same time, there is a natural adjustment in the wrists to accommodate the lie of the club; our wrists bend according to the lie. Meanwhile, we bend easily from the waist in order to set the club.

When setting up over the ball, we follow this procedure: first, we walk into the starting form by setting the clubface behind the ball with the ball placed toward the toe end of the clubhead.

Simultaneously, we set the right foot at right angles to the target. The shaft runs straight up and down, as designed, and rests in the midpoint of our stance. We then establish the position of the left foot while assuming a natural flex in our legs and a natural bend from the waist. We then form the grip. This is the starting form, except for ball location and posture.

Ball location relative to the left foot and alignment.

BALL LOCATION

This is a critical aspect of the starting position that we often ignore or misunderstand. It's not complicated. We want to find a location for the ball relative to our stance so that the ball will get in the way of the clubhead on its way to the finish position. Since the swing is an uninterrupted motion along a definite path, all we need to do is find the location for the ball that will ensure it is sent off accurately, and with proper distance and trajectory. Golf is not a hand-eye game, so it stands to reason that we should find a location for the ball that will not vary from shot to shot.

Ball location flows logically from the way we set up in the starting position. The arms and hands hang naturally as we grip the club. There's no reason to move them forward, that is, toward the left foot. Neither is there any reason to move them back, toward the right foot. They quite naturally hang just ahead of the middle of the stance. We place the ball, then, just ahead of the middle of the stance for a standard five-iron shot. The ball, then, will be just back of the inside of the left heel.

Now, the width of the stance will vary with the length of the club. The longer the club, the wider the stance. It is in the interests of consistency that we keep the left foot in a constant position relative to the ball location. We move the right foot only as we set up, closer or further from the left foot depending on the club we have in our hands. The right foot is furthest away from the left foot when we are using a driver. But the position of the left foot relative to the ball is constant. We thereby ensure a constant ball position.

The other reason for maintaining a constant position for the left foot relative to the ball is that we want to finish flat on that foot. It's where we're headed. The destination does not change, so neither should the position of the left foot or the ball location.

While the position of the left foot does not change relative to the ball, the distance we stand from the ball does. As I said, I feel different every day. When I go to the range, I want to find a place for the ball that allows me to feel comfortable while I set up and swing. If I'm feeling particularly flexible, I might put the ball out a half-inch or so.

If I'm tight that day, I might move it a little closer. It all depends on how I feel. I'm a stickler on balance, and so I'm not going to do anything that makes me feel uneasy. Neither should you. Experiment with the distance the ball is from your stance until you find the place from which you can swing freely and hit the ball straight. That's your ball location for the day.

The most efficient means of setting the starting position relative to the ball is this: set the clubhead to the ball location, then set the body around the club. You therefore work your body off your target. Should we do otherwise, we are likely to set up a visual distortion. It's

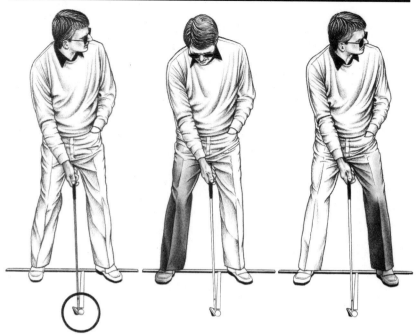

Square the clubface
to the target.

Square the right foot
to the target.

Set the left foot open
to the target.

much more efficient to move the body around the clubface rather than the other way around. It's so much easier (and so much less subject to error) to aim your clubface accurately than to aim your body. The clubface then acts as a reference point. We may become confused if we orient the body to the target; it's got too many parts.

The golfer who arranges his body first and the clubface second endangers good form. He will automatically try to correct physically for the visual distortion he's fallen victim to. That's why golfers are often convinced that they're aligned properly when in reality they may be well off line. But they've gotten used to a certain way of setting up. I found this out when I was sixteen years old; it took me up to a week to correct myself.

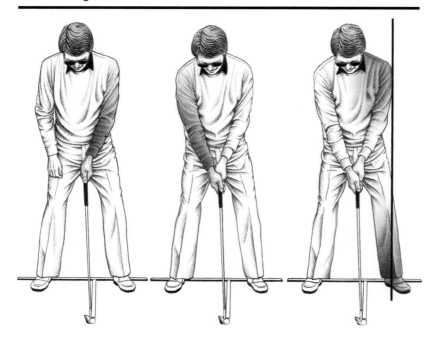

Set the left hand on the club.

Set the right hand on the club.

Ensure the left foot is open and outside the left shoulder. Notice that the shoulders are open to the target.

Jack Nicklaus's teacher Jack Grout makes the point very well about the importance of proper alignment. He tells of watching Nicklaus prior to a round in the 1974 U.S. Open at Winged Foot Golf Club in Mamaroneck, N.Y. Nicklaus, it seems, was hitting the ball worse than he ever had. It was all due to his very closed shoulder alignment; the trouble was that Nicklaus didn't know it. He had compensated for his sloppy alignment by re-routing his swing. Since he was doing so subconsciously,

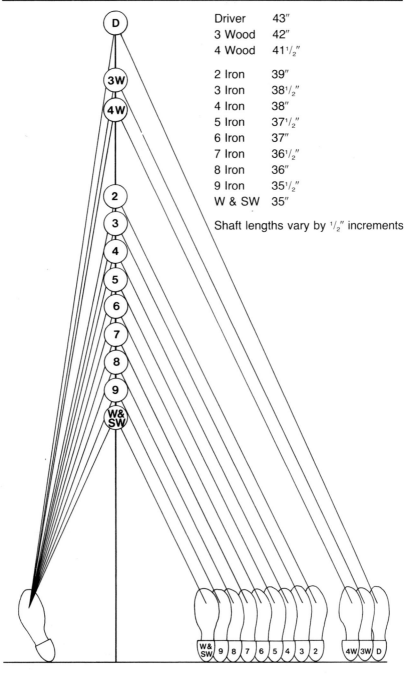

Driver	43″
3 Wood	42″
4 Wood	41½″
2 Iron	39″
3 Iron	38½″
4 Iron	38″
5 Iron	37½″
6 Iron	37″
7 Iron	36½″
8 Iron	36″
9 Iron	35½″
W & SW	35″

Shaft lengths vary by ½″ increments

Left foot is constant

Width of stance varies
by ½″ increments from club to club

he had no way of correcting himself. Nicklaus thought he was setting up down the centre of the fairway, but he was aimed out-of-bounds to the right.

Grout saw Nicklaus again a few days later at the Muirfield Village Golf Club in Dublin, Ohio. Nicklaus was still setting up far to the right with his shoulders closed. Grout turned him around properly, even a bit open, as the shoulders should be, but Nicklaus had gotten so used to his misshapen alignment that he refused to believe he could get the ball in the fairway from the position Grout had put him in. Grout told him, effectively, "Trust me. Swing."

Nicklaus swung all right. Every ball flew straight down the middle. The greatest player in the world hadn't known that he was aligning himself improperly. He needed another pair of eyes to help him see his mistake. Until Grout corrected him, Nicklaus had been compensating physically for his visual distortion.

I mention the Nicklaus story to point out the importance of accurate alignment. Always be on the lookout for any laziness that creeps into your set-up. If you go wrong here, you will go wrong elsewhere. Start in a good position, as I must emphasize, and you'll help ensure that you'll finish in a good position; the result you desire will be the inevitable by-product.

POSTURE

The length and lie of the golf club determine our posture in the starting position. We want to stand as tall as we can. We neither stretch to the ball nor reach for it.

Take a five-iron in your hand and grip it as instructed. Place it on the ground so that the sole lies flat. Now, simply bend slightly from the waist to allow the arms to hang in a natural extension. Your knees will flex a bit as you do so.

Proper posture is proud posture. If you stand to the ball
comfortably and in good height
you will pre-set the conditions
for attaining a maximum arc
during the motion.

Arc is the perimeter of the
swing, as defined by the line the
clubhead traces through its path
during the motion. You could
define the arc if you were to
trace the line of that perimeter.
All we want to do is ensure that
the arc is never less than maximum throughout the motion. It's
easy to repeat a maximum arc
because there is then no question
as to swinging in an intermedi-
ate space. Imagine that you are
driving on a ring road around
a city. The road can be represented as an arc. You know you
need only stay on this road to
reach a certain destination, or
exit. But you might get lost if
you went inside the ring, into the
congested city space. You might
also get lost if you travelled
outside the ring, that is, beyond
the arc. And this would result
in a loss of balance.

The starting form.

The arc in the golf swing is the ring road, as measured by its distance from the centre. Stay on it and you will be consistent. Vary from it and you court inconsistency.

Anything less than a maximum arc is an out-of-balance condition. A maximum arc is a matter of elevation and posture throughout the swing, along with extension. And we can construct the foundation for this in the starting position.

You'll give yourself your best chance for a maximum arc if you let your arms hang in the starting position. They'll stretch to their maximum as you swing. They'll also move along at a reasonable and correct pace since there's neither restriction nor resistance.

One more item: it's important that you evaluate your starting position every time you prepare to make a swing. Here's a check list:
  Proper grip
  Hands opposing
  Proper stance
  Proper alignment
  Your best posture
  Natural, relaxed arm extension
  Proper weight distribution

Practise the starting form whenever you can. Think about balance and the elements will fall into place. Get the grip, stance, alignment, and posture right and you'll be well on your way to developing a natural swing motion. You'll be a well-organized golfer. You'll have arranged the preliminary items in such a way that you'll have a splendid chance of getting the job done. It's amazing how much progress a formerly confused golfer can make just by getting the starting position right. It really sets him up. It really makes him feel like a golfer. And balance is the key. If we don't understand balance we have no basis from which to operate. Everything in the natural swing motion derives from balance.

6. Loading: The Backswing Motion

BEFORE beginning the swing motion, let's review the reasoning behind the starting form. Since the golf swing is one unified motion, it's fair to say that the starting form is a lead-in. It sets the tone of harmony and ease. It asks nothing of you but a sense of balance and proportion. You're now ready to make an efficient motion. The starting form gives you a chance to execute properly.

Why do I prefer to call the backswing a loading motion? I believe the word "backswing" alone suggests that we *take* the club back to a position. It implies that it is a discrete part of the swing. Certainly it is convenient to divide the swing into the backswing and downswing portions, but I differ with the idea that these are two separate actions. They aren't, as we will see. In fact, the unloading motion begins while we are still in the loading motion.

The term "loading" seems to me a useful one. It implies energy and commitment. The very tone of the word gives you the feeling that something is going to happen, something vigorous and energizing.

Weight transfer and trunk rotation.

The purpose of the loading motion is to gather energy. We do so by transferring weight to the right foot while rotating the body around the trunk. These actions seem to happen in unison, but in reality we initiate the motion with a shift of weight toward the right foot. The upper body and shoulders pick up the beat almost immediately and follow. The feet carry the body, as in walking. It's important to understand that there need not be any sense of urgency in loading.

We want to feel relaxed. Transfer weight and let the energy accumulate. This will generate a pleasant feeling in which we feel connected; a far different sensation than if we were to initiate the motion by picking the club up. This, of course, would immediately ruin balance and compromise arc and plane.

We have completed the loading motion when approximately seventy-five per cent of our weight is on our right side. I say seventy-five per cent because it is impossible to shift a hundred per cent of our weight to the right side without losing balance. The loading motion is also less of a rotation than the unloading motion, and so some twenty-five per cent of our weight remains forward of the right foot. While loading, we rotate through ninety degrees; while unloading, we rotate through 180 degrees.

It might appear that during the loading motion the clubhead is travelling first, followed by the hands, shoulders, hips, knees, and finally the left foot. However, all parts are moving together. It just so happens that the clubhead is travelling further than the hands, shoulders, hips, knees, and the left foot. Everything is moving in unison.

Fully loaded.

that is dependent upon your sensitivity to balance and your awareness of your target. Let me explain.

Centrifugal force will have carried the club a good distance; as far, in fact, as it need go. You don't have to worry about reaching that much-talked about position where the clubshaft is level to the ground with the clubhead pointing down the target line. The force propels the club to a position that represents an outer limit for *you*, given your flexibility. Were you not practising the natural swing governed by laws of motion and balance, you might think you should carry the club further back; or perhaps drop it to what you think is a level-to-the-ground position. (Golfers mean this when they ask: "Have I

You might wonder how you know that you have completed the loading motion. After all, you haven't got a scale that tells you when you have shifted seventy -five per cent of your weight rearward. The indicator is a sixth sense that you will develop and

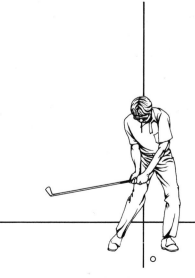

reached parallel?'') They are referring to the level-to-the-ground position. Such maneuvers are superfluous. They create a false sense of security because they take place *after* you have completed the loading motion. The loading motion is over when centrifugal force has taken you as far as you can go while maintaining balance. You'll soon learn and become sensitive to any extra manipulations. You'll realize that you are letting yourself get out of balance. Let the club flow. That's the key word: LET.

The intensity of your target awareness will also contribute to your sense of when you have completed the loading motion. It operates in conjunction with your sensitivity to balance. You know that your objective is to make a motion toward the target. You've fixed the image of the target on your mind's eye. And since you are so aware of the target, you also sense when it is time to start moving toward it, that is, to begin the unloading motion. This will happen sometime toward the end of the loading motion, which is why I say that loading and unloading are part of the same motion.

Consider this: centrifugal force and inertia are allowing you to make a pure, uninterrupted swing motion. As you are carried back, having a free ride, really, you sense that it is time to move to your target. To do otherwise would be to compromise balance. Your intent to move to the target and your acute sense of balance ensure that you won't go too far while loading. You'll know when it's time to start the unloading motion just as you know when you've gotten out of balance while climbing a hill. Golfers are surprised at how sensitive they can become to their own errors; but it's a sensitivity we all have.

The end of the loading motion comes, then, when the mass has developed all the potential energy it wants, under the condition of balance. You sense when this has occurred, and so you begin the unloading motion.

You begin the unloading motion, then, while still loading. Your target awareness induces you to do so. If you weren't focusing on your target, you would have no reason to complete the loading motion. You might very well continue back, where you would dissipate all the energy you accumulated through weight transfer and rotation. Target awareness is the stimulant that helps you click in to the latter part of the loading motion and the initiation of the unloading motion. The clubhead changes direction because you have transferred weight to the finish position.

Let's examine the loading motion more closely. We'll look at what you need to learn and what happens on its own: the voluntary and the involuntary, as I like to call these skills and actions.

First, we have assumed a starting position in which we are oriented toward our target. We're in place; we've pre-determined the arc and plane. We now need to set ourselves in motion in such a way that we will maximize the arc and remain on-plane.

We initiate the swing motion by shifting weight to our right foot. This is the means of moving the clubhead. When we walk, we don't shake or turn our upper body. The upper body follows the beat of the legs.

We are aware of our balance and posture, and to maintain these elements we allow ourselves to rotate around the trunk.

Our hands are passive or quiet, but actually set in motion by weight transfer and rotation.

''Passive hands'' is not meant to suggest inactive hands. It's just that we don't consciously do anything with them.

But how do we keep the hands out of the swing? Aren't they lively devils that want to get into the act? Aren't they our only connections to the club? Doesn't that mean we should *do* something with them?

This is precisely the point. Our hands will be as active as we need them to be if we *let* them move along with the rest of the body.

For the moment, pick up a golf club and address an imaginary ball. Let your weight go from your left foot to your right foot. Did you notice that your hands moved along with the weight shift? And they moved in a pure path. You didn't have to *put* them anywhere. They went along for the ride. A golfer can do marvellous things with his feet. I believe in playing golf through your feet. Footwork is the voluntary action that initiates the motion. So send a message to your feet. Put yourself in motion through weight transfer; develop your sense of balance so that you know when you've gone beyond the inside of your right foot. If you feel yourself getting out of balance, you are no longer transferring weight. You're swaying. A sway is an imbalance. Keep the weight to the inside of the right foot while rotating.

The loading motion is generally circular in shape. Instead of transferring our weight so far that we lose balance, we simply let ourselves rotate around our trunk. I'm describing this as if it were separate from the weight transfer, but in reality the weight transfer and rotation happen almost simultaneously. All parts of the body move more or less in unison during the loading motion.

I say "more or less" because I find that the most effective means of beginning the loading motion is through my footwork. As soon as I start the weight shift, though, my upper body cannot help but follow. I therefore transfer weight while rotating; I rotate while transferring weight.

The loading motion.
Top left, left arm extends, right elbow folds. *Top right*, head moving as it will. *Centre*, natural wrist cock. *Bottom left*, left heel comes up during rotation. *Bottom right*, full rotation.

Fully loaded, immaculate balance.

The effect of the motion is to allow the hands to work in tandem with the clubhead. They just travel along, and what a relief it is not to have to think about them. We need not worry about our hands.

The loading motion, then, is a matter of moving immediately to the right foot. Feel the ground under your feet. Feel your weight go to your right foot. As we do shift weight under the governance of balance, our hands remain passive, and the left arm extends naturally. The right elbow folds on the way back as long as the hands are passive. These are involuntary or automatic responses to the motion. The wrists cock as a result of the mass of the club being put in motion by the weight transfer while loading. This too is an automatic action, as is the wrist cock that happens at the completion of the loading motion.

The voluntary actions in the loading motion that you need to learn are weight transfer and rotation; that is, you *make* these happen. The involuntary or automatic actions or positions are: the right elbow folding and the left arm extending, thereby creating a maximum arc during loading; the head moving as it will; the wrists cocking; the left heel coming up off the ground as you shift weight; the back turned more or less to where it is facing the target at the completion of loading, depending on your flexibility.

We've now reached the top of the loading motion. Centrifugal force and inertia have taken us to a powerful and balanced position. We're in balance and intent on our target. It's time to begin the unloading motion.

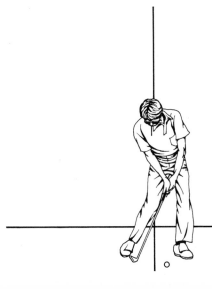

7. Unloading: The Downswing Motion

FOR PURPOSES of explanation, we distinguish the loading and unloading motions from each other. They are actually part of the same motion. We begin to unload the power we have developed while we are still completing the loading motion.

The intent to transfer weight to the finishing position generates a sequence of motion. The left foot is the first part of the body to stabilize, or find its finishing or resting place. Depending on a person's flexibility, it will have come up off the ground to a certain degree during the loading motion. Now, as the golfer transfers weight to the finishing position, the left foot returns to the ground. It takes the weight of the body.

Following the stabilization of the left foot are the left knee, then the hips, the shoulders,

arms, hands, and finally the clubhead. These reach their natural end points because we have transferred weight while unloading.

Simultaneous with the weight shift, some remarkable things take place without you trying to make them happen. The clubhead begins to lag behind your feet and body, a natural reaction to centrifugal force. This natural happening is known as clubhead delay or clubhead lag. It is an

involuntary response to the force that put the clubhead into a powerful position at the end of the loading motion, and to your intent to transfer weight to the finishing position.

Your right arm, as indicated, straightens during unloading from its folded position while loading. Your weight transfer to the finishing position while in balance and with full extension – due to your starting form of relaxed shoulders, arms, and hands – ensures that this occurs. You are allowing the arc to be maximized. You don't need to do a thing for this to happen; just allow it to happen.

The unloading motion begins when we transfer the body weight to the finishing position. We transfer weight from the right foot to the left foot, the two pivot points in the swing motion. This causes a number of very good things to happen during the unloading motion. These are, of course, involuntary. They *happen* because we transfer weight.

First, the wrists are put in a maximum cocked position due to the weight transfer to the finishing position.

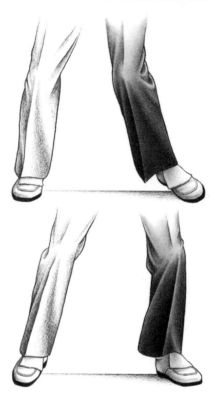

Top, position of the left foot at the completion of the loading motion. *Bottom,* stabilization of the left foot during unloading.

At impact, the arms become fully extended while the hands and wrists return to their natural form, that is, square to the target for a straight shot. The right elbow, meanwhile, returns to an extended form at impact.

Beyond impact, the left elbow will fold midway to the finishing position while the right arm extends. The right elbow will fold

Involuntary hand action before impact, at impact, and after impact.

at the completion of the swing motion.

The unloading motion is truly a simple, responsive act. It's a matter of trusting that what has come before is correct; if you set up the starting form correctly and then make the swing motion I'm presenting here, you can be sure it *is* correct.

Give up control to gain control. I've said it before and I'll say it again. There's no need to force things in the natural swing. Just let yourself be.

You'll have flowed through to a complete, graceful finishing form because you won't have interfered with the motion.

8. The Finishing Form

THE FINISHING FORM is one in which you face the target at natural, full height. Your body faces the target – feet, knees, hips, shoulders, torso, shoulders, and head – and all of your weight is on your left foot. There's a natural flex in your left knee, while your right knee is also flexed. Your right foot, having shifted forward due to the weight transfer to your left foot, has come up.

Given that you have not controlled the club at all during the motion, it will now flow where it may, probably completing its travels somewhere behind your back. We don't care where it goes; centrifugal force carries the club until it has spent its energy. At the same time, the hands and wrists are in the same form as at the start.

I once asked a thirteen-year-old gymnast in Halifax why she committed herself so fully to her sport. "Because I feel so free when I do it," she answered. And that's a feeling you will have as you move through to assume the proper finishing form. You can't help but notice the feeling of freedom as you let yourself go to the finish.

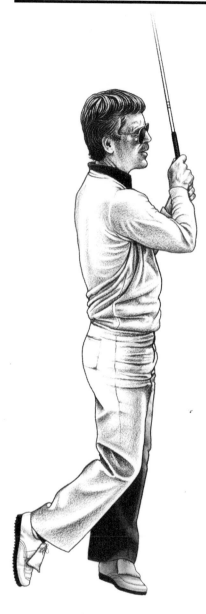

The finishing position, all the weight on the left foot.

You're following through on every linked aspect of the motion that came before. Not that you're trying to. You know the difference between trying and enabling, between forcing and allowing. You're going along for the ride.

It's important to understand that the finishing position is truly a *form*. It's true that you get to the position by allowing the motion to take place. But you also help yourself immeasurably in reaching the position by having a picture of the form in your mind's eye from the beginning. Now that you understand the motion, you can appreciate why it's critical that you visualize from the beginning the form you will assume at the end. As I said earlier with respect to the positioning of the left foot, it's important to know where you're going if you plan to arrive there.

Where are you going? What do you want to visualize? How will you look?

You are moving to a point where you will stand with one hundred per cent of your weight on your left foot, your body facing the target in perfect balance. It makes sense that you

Let's look more closely at the by-the-way, involuntary happenings that take place as you move to the finishing position. The more confident you feel that these happen on their own due to the natural swing motion, the more easily you will let it all happen.

First, your left elbow folds midway toward the finishing position as the heaviness in the mass pulls you along and around to face the target. Your commitment to face the target will pull your right leg slightly forward. This is because your intent is to transfer one hundred per cent of your weight to your left foot in order to conform to the principle of balance. Your right foot will just be hanging at the finishing position. You won't miss

Top, transferring the weight to the left foot.
Bottom, the right foot at the finish.

are moving to this position. If you're moving forward by transferring weight to the left foot, then you want to let all the weight go. Anything else suggests restriction; and this is an imbalance. Instead, you intend to let all the energy go.

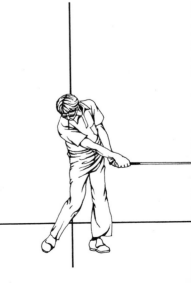

Various finish positions for different shots, all in balance.

this position if you have made a total weight transfer. Your right leg will slide forward as all of your weight moves to the left foot, and will stabilize at a point halfway to your right foot. Since you are moving to a position of full height in which all of your weight is on your left foot, your right foot will also come up. At the finish your right foot will, as indicated, hang. This is a clear indication that you have shifted all your weight forward, and that you have indeed moved from one pivot point –

the right foot – to the other pivot point – the left foot. At the same time, your right knee will move forward and then in toward the left knee. It will finish beside your left knee; they will nearly touch one another. These positions cannot help but come about if you are in balance. You will get to these positions if the form is right.

What about the golf club? It's simply gone off on its own path. The club will, as mentioned, likely travel to a point behind your back. This is an automatic response. You'll recall that the arms, hands, and wrists have remained passive from the start, and that you began while holding the golf club in front of you. You haven't severed the connections you started with. The club has travelled all the way around with your body. You haven't interfered with it. Just let the club go where it's going to go. It's the body form that counts. When you're finished, having been in balance throughout, you'll be standing in a perfectly relaxed form. Your arms will have dropped to the desirable and relaxed recessed position. I like to call this position the ''best seat in the house.'' This is the place from where you evaluate your form and enjoy the result. Eventually your arms will get to the desirable and relaxed recessed position.

You must evaluate your finishing form. Many golfers pay some attention to their starting form, but few have a good look at the finishing form. They think that because the ball has been struck, the swing is over. So why bother examining the finishing form?

Evaluation of the
finishing form.

NATURAL HEIGHT

FACING TARGET

IN BALANCE

MAINTAINING HAND
AND WRIST FORMATION

The way you finish can give
you many clues as to how you
arrived there. That's why I want
you to take a good look. It's
easier to do so if you allow your
arms to drop to a recessed position in front of your chest. They
will have travelled along with
the club to a point above or
slightly behind your left shoulder. If you're relaxed, then your
arms will drop naturally to the
recessed position. This happens
no matter what type of shot you
are playing. There are times
that you may not go all the way
to the finishing position you
reach on a full swing; this happens, for instance, when you
hit less than a full shot. But the
club still has a mind of its own.
Momentum determines the
breadth of the motion. We don't
control it.

You can now evaluate. Where is your weight? Is it all on your front foot? Have you held anything back? Do you feel yourself tilting right or left? If you do, this means you didn't transfer your weight evenly on to your left foot; all your weight should be evenly distributed across your foot if you are in balance. Similarly, notice if you have rolled to the outside of your left foot, or if you didn't reach the position where one hundred per cent of your weight should be. Either condition means that you set up improperly. Check the angle of the left foot relative to the target. This determines direction. Also check the location of the left foot relative to the left shoulder. The left foot must be outside the left shoulder to establish proper balance.

It's important to evaluate after each swing motion. Are you in balance? Are you in natural height? Are you facing the target? Have you maintained the hand and wrist formation? I got to the point where I knew it if I was just a hair out of balance. You *can* become that sensitive.

You *can* get to the point when it will shock you if you do something to disturb balance. It won't be something you have to look for. You will *know* it.

I want to stress the importance of evaluation of your finishing form. It really does complete the motion. It turns every swing motion into a separate learning opportunity. It's the best way to achieve that much-sought-after state of concentrating on each shot and playing one shot at a time. It helps put you into a concentrated state. It also reduces anxiety by taking your mind off the result. It's not what you do that counts. It's what you attempt to do.

We're concerned with the long run. That's why we evaluate each swing motion. We intend to play golf for a long time, and so we take the long-term view. Paradoxically, we facilitate a long-term view by evaluating each and every swing motion, one at a time. Then we forget it. We learn as we go along because we are not interfering with the learning process by interjecting value judgments. It's simply evaluation, integration of information, and then onto the next swing motion. It takes time to learn and change. And so we give ourselves time.

Ben Hogan was a brilliant evaluator. He assessed each swing very carefully. He wanted to give himself the best chance of not making the same mistake again, or, conversely, of doing the right thing again. Every swing is an object lesson. Every swing that you evaluate is an opportunity gained. Every swing that you don't evaluate is an opportunity lost.

Evaluation and assessment are crucial. These procedures help make golf a logical game. We learn where our good and bad shots come from.

You've now learned the starting and finishing forms. You've learned the means of motion and the laws and principles that apply. You understand the swing as a motion. You know that golf is a target game.

In the next chapter I'd like to go through many of the misconceptions we've absorbed over the years. They have no place in the natural swing. You can now appreciate that if an idea, tip, or theory disturbs balance, then it has no place in golf.

9. An End to Misconceptions

GOLF IS FULL of misconceptions that we've taken for truth. We're so eager to improve that we'll try anything.

The misconceptions that follow are a direct result of the fact that most golf theory has ignored the aspect of motion. Now that you understand that the swing is a motion that conforms to the laws of motion, it will be easy for you to understand where the misconceptions came from. You will also be able to ignore them for the rest of your golfing days.

Gene Sarazen was once asked what he does when he swings. "I ride through the ball," he answered. That's a powerful image. It tells us so much about the swing as motion. We're free. We want to move without restrictions.

Balance, as we know, is the key fundamental to the natural golf swing. It's the singular essential, the one factor we think about and the major condition that we evaluate. To be in balance is to be relaxed, in a state of equilibrium. Yet much of what we are told to do during the golf swing would put us out-of-balance, not to mention out of commission sometimes. Doctors' and chiropractors' offices are full of golfers who have contorted themselves into such

convoluted shapes that they can hardly get out of bed, let alone make a swing motion.

Golf instruction is full of misconceptions and misinformation, including good ideas that have been garbled and misinterpreted as they've come into common usage. For instance, it's a good idea to develop maximum extension. But it's not a good idea to throw the club behind you so that you can almost put it in your back pocket. You lose energy that way. Yet many golfers think that extension means just that: sticking the club behind their backs. That might ease an itch, but it won't do anything for extension.

And yet we accept the ill-conceived information. It's as if we have looked at the golf swing through a pair of glasses with a particular prescription: "Follow these rules of thumb and you can't go wrong." But how can they be right if they violate balance? How can they be correct if they result in us overworking our bodies? The golf swing is much easier and much more enjoyable than we have been taught. We want to retain and develop energy, not lose it. An imbalanced condition strips us of our energy.

You will be familiar with most or all of the following misconceptions. I'll examine each of them with respect to the natural golf swing. Then we can ignore them, forever.

Grip the Club Firmly

I was as guilty of this as anybody. I used to hold the club as if I were in a tug-of-war. I thought that "death-gripping" the club was the way to ensure that I wouldn't lose control of it. Of course, the only thing I accomplished was to tense the muscles in my hands, forearms, and shoulders.

Don't bother with the death-grip. Ignore the articles that tell you to hold on tightly with the last three fingers of the left hand. It's true that the pressure is in the last three fingers, but you don't *make* that happen. It happens as a result of the compact grip you assume as part of the natural form.

Also stay away from other variations on the theme, as in: to grip firmly with the middle two fingers of the right hand and/or the thumb and forefinger of the right hand.

Hold the club no more firmly than you would a butterfly or a baby. You want to feel the club in your hands. You need soft hands to do that.

Keep the Left Arm Straight

The size of the arc during the loading motion is defined by the length of the left arm plus the club. Golf instructors have long known that when the left arm is most extended, the golfer is most likely to have developed both a source of power – a maximum arc – and a source of accuracy (an arc that because it is maximized can be repeated). Unfortunately, instructors have taught that the golfer should therefore keep his left arm straight. He is told to force it straight, to extend it on his own.

Straightening the left arm has the effect of tensing it. It is, in effect, a hyperextension that interferes with natural extension and in the process introduces tension and rigidity.

Golfers have observed others at the top of the backswing and seen a straight left arm. They have examined stop-action photographs of better players and seen a straight left arm. But it is an effect, not a cause.

The left arm will extend on its own if the grip is relaxed in the starting form and during the swing. Centrifugal force and inertia will extend the muscles naturally. Transfer weight and you'll have all the extension you need. You need not do a thing to extend it.

When Gripping the Club, Point the V's Toward the Right Shoulder

This idea must have arisen to compensate for the torque or twist in the old hickory shafts. Golfers must have felt that by pointing the V's toward the right shoulder they would have a better chance of getting the clubface squarely on the ball. Applied to steel shafts, and given the balance requirement, this is a distortion. The golfer who points the V's toward the right shoulder and then makes a pure swing will

hook the ball wildly as his hands turn over at impact due to weight transfer. They will have rotated too much during the downswing.

The hands must oppose one another symmetrically in order to maintain balance in the starting form. Centrifugal force will return the hands to this position through impact. This will happen of its own accord. Let it happen.

Sit on the Seat Stick
This posture-related rule of thumb destroys posture. It's in the same category as the admonition to sit down to the ball as if you're taking a place on a bar stool. The effect is to compress the golfer; how can you maintain maximum elevation, and therefore encourage a maximum arc, if at address you're already sitting down, with your weight back?

You will put yourself in good posture when you let the length and lie of the club determine your elevation at address. Place the clubhead behind the ball so that the sole is flat on the ground. Then bend as you need to keep it there.

Address the Ball With Your Left Arm and Shaft in a Straight Line
This is another distortion of a balanced starting position. It introduces tension into the left arm and upper back. It pulls the left shoulder up and out (toward the ball) and the right shoulder down and back. It pushes your weight forward, destroying the fifty-fifty distribution of weight during the starting position that we want between the right and left feet – the two pivot points.

This misconception is associated with the "keep-your-left-arm-straight" idea. It is meant to promote extension. But it prevents good form. All we're trying to do at address is give ourselves the best chance of making a pure motion. What chance have we got if we're contorted at the start?

Keep the Weight on the Insides of Your Feet
Any person who stands on the ground with his weight distributed toward the insides of his feet is out of balance. If you'll stand up now, your weight will be evenly distributed between your feet. There's no point in distributing the weight otherwise on a flat surface. This doesn't

change because you have a golf club in your hands.

Pinching the feet in pinches the knees in and tenses the legs. It forces attention upon the lower body because you are now uncomfortable and unnatural. You'll subconsciously feel that you want to get your weight back flat on your feet, evenly distributed. This focus on one area will inevitably disrupt the calm, even feeling you want throughout your body in the starting position. This misconception, like so many, developed from the admonition to keep your head still.

Keep the Weight Toward Your Heels

This will assist you greatly if your intent is to tilt and perhaps fall over during the swing. The golfer who leans back at address is a golfer who slips and slides during the swing. You want to feel active while relaxed at address. Keeping the weight toward the heels encourages slumping. This is a drowsy position from which to begin a vigorous motion. Avoid it by setting up in a balanced position.

Bend the Knees

Absolutely no good can come from bending the knees. Golfers who do so not only look awkward, they pitch their bodies forward as if somebody has shoved them from behind. The effect is also to push weight into the feet and then into the ground. The knees will bend a discrete and proper amount as you fit into your starting position. You don't need to add any flex to what comes naturally.

Chin Up at Address

This is a misguided attempt to ensure you'll be able to make a shoulder turn. The hope is that by keeping your chin up you will create room for your left shoulder as you make your backswing. The difficulty here is that you will create tension in the back of your neck that will likely restrict your shoulder turn.

You want to feel "oily" at address. Sam Snead used this term to describe how he felt throughout his swing and I can't imagine a better image. Set up as I have indicated in previous chapters and you won't have any need to thrust your chin up. When you are in natural posture, your chin will be just where it should be.

Set Up With Your Right Elbow Lower Than Your Left

This popular notion derives from an adjustment golfers think they must make due to the placement of the right hand on the club. The right hand is then obviously lower than the left. This opens the shoulders to the target. There's nothing the matter with this. Our anatomy does it.

Some golf teachers, however, are determined to make their pupils arrange their hands, arms, and shoulders in a perfect triangle. So they advise the pupil to go against nature by sticking his right arm into the side of his chest. This is supposed to square up the shoulders, hips, and knees. However, it's not a balanced position. You may as

well squeeze yourself into an overcrowded elevator for all the discomfort and muscular tension you'll feel. Remember, we relax to play golf. Tucking the right elbow in ensures maximum discomfort, not maximum ease. It means that we'll have to manipulate the golf club and our bodies during the swing: and there goes the motion.

So let the arms hang. Square to the target, as we've learned, is slightly open.

Keep the Head Down

This is the number one misconception concerning the swing. It's also expressed as "keep your head still," or "keep your eye on the ball." The idea of keeping the head still and the eye on the ball has everything to do with the mistaken belief that golf is a hand-eye game: and if it is, then we'd better keep our eye on the ball. This, of course, leads to the notion that the head is the pivot point of the swing, the one part that does not move. In other words, we fear that if it does move, we'll mis-hit the ball, or worse, miss it entirely.

Golfers who are mesmerized by the ball feel they have to hit it rather than swing through it.

That means keeping the head locked. But all that does is lock up the body.

Hitting the ball is not the answer. Golf is *not* a hand-eye game. The idea is to stay relaxed and let the centrifugal force extend the arms, hands, and club downward and outward to create a maximum arc in the swing motion.

Body location relative to ball location will determine the contact between clubhead and ball. It is body location relative to the ball in the starting form rather than hand-eye coordination that is the key factor in making solid contact. The answer and the fun lie in creating a free-swinging motion that will meet the ball on the way to the target.

This misconception has done more harm to more golf swings than any piece of advice I've come across. It wrecks balance, for one thing. We see a golfer's head behind the ball at impact and we think it's there because he's kept it down or still throughout his swing. This is a misperception. We're seeing an effect, not a cause. If he's swung freely, he's swung in motion and in balance. His head has merely returned to impact with the rest of his body.

We restrict motion right from the start when we keep the head still. We thereby carry so much weight in our heads. It is a principle of motion that we move with a light head, with a head balanced softly on our necks.

Try this experiment with a partner. Lie on your back. Have your partner sit behind you in a comfortable position while sliding his hands under your head from the front. Let him gradually move his hands under your head so that he is supporting the head. Focus your attention on dropping the weight of your head into his hands. As you release the weight, your partner will gently lift your head a couple of inches off the floor. Continue to allow the weight of your head to sink into his hands.

Imagine that your head would drop to the floor if he let go, which of course he won't. Your partner might want to move your head around a bit; this introduction of motion will let you drop more of the weight of your head into his hands. Your partner will then guide your head back to the floor, and remove his hands.

Notice how light-headed you feel. Do you have a sensation of freedom in your head? We carry so much weight in parts of our body, yet are quite accustomed to doing so. We don't realize it can be different. And the head, of course, is the heaviest part of our body relative to other parts. If we hold it rigidly during the golf swing, we make it even heavier. It's meant to move as we move. The simple exercise I have given here will demonstrate how much weight we hold in our head when we keep it still.

There are so many things we cannot do if we keep the head still. We cannot transfer weight naturally, for one. There must be movement throughout if there's going to be a weight transfer. That's natural motion.

If there is any sense that anything is nailed down or restricted, if we're doing anything to take away the freedom, then it becomes an unnatural motion.

The head is not the pivot point of the golf swing. The feet are the pivot points. You transfer weight from foot to foot. The head travels where the body takes it during the swing motion. It will do so when we think of balance. The head moves as we displace weight while loading and unloading during the swing. It goes back and forth and up and down, wherever it wants. The body carries the head.

A final word on the absurdity of keeping the head still. We've been led to believe that golf can hurt the back. There's supposed to be such a condition as the "golfer's back." If golfers do develop bad backs, the condition is often due to keeping their head still. It forces them to swing the club away from the ball while staying in one place, and then to swing through it while doing the same. If you keep your head still while swinging away from the ball – particularly if your intent is to hit the ball – then your feet will

remain locked in place; to coun-
teract your movement away from
the ball and to allow yourself
to keep the head still, you may
even find your lower body moving forward during the backswing, the classic reverse pivot.
The opposite thing might happen
on the throughswing, your weight
moving back as you move forward. No wonder golfers wreck
their backs. Keeping the head
still causes what has become
known as the ''Reverse C'' finish position, in which the golfer
retards the forward motion of
his upper body in an effort to
maintain his rigid head position.
Is this natural? Can this be right?

**Take Club Back Low and Slow
(Take Club Back in a Straight
Line)**
Here the golfer is warned against
lifting the club as he starts the
backswing, or what I call the
loading motion. The idea does
encourage width in the arc, but
unfortunately the wording causes
golfers to emphasize the ''low
and slow'' aspect while ignoring
the important roles weight transfer and rotation play in moving
the club back. The club goes
back low and slow if the golfer
initiates his motion through foot-

work. Initiation with the hands
induces, rather than prevents,
quickness and lifting.

This suggestion can also result
in the dreaded reverse pivot. A
golfer who pays attention to this
tip is prone to dragging the club
back along the ground. He'll
probably get stuck on his feet;
he'll have introduced very little
lower-body motion by the time
he has swung the club back low
and slow.

If you think about it, ''straight
back'' is geometrically impossible because of the pitch of the
plane as set up in the starting
form. The club must travel on a
generally circular route.

You promote a smooth takeaway by refining your footwork
on the takeaway in combination
with rotation and passive hands.

The club will track as low and slow as it needs to before turning round your body as trunk rotation takes it there.

The Longer the Swing, the Further the Ball Will Fly. Length of Swing = Distance

It's true that a longer swing will result in more distance than a shorter swing. A bigger arc will result in a greater build-up of clubhead speed. This is why I've always said that I couldn't beat Tom Weiskopf if we were both playing to the maximum of our abilities. He's 6'3" and I'm 5'10". He's bound to hit the ball further, all other swing-motion conditions being equal. He simply has more arc.

Notice that I said, "all other swing-motion conditions being equal." I am assuming we would both be making the best use of the fundamentals of the natural golf swing. And since Weiskopf's swing is longer than mine, he will generate more length. His height advantage will produce a greater circumference to his arc. He has room to build up more centrifugal force. But should he merely swing the club back a good distance without

moving his body, he would develop very little energy. If this were the case, then, I would hit the ball further than he would.

Energy develops when the swing motion creates maximum extension under the conditions of weight transfer and rotation. We dissipate energy when we swing the clubhead. By all means, swing longer, but with your body, not your hands. Make an honest swing motion, not an ineffectual swing.

Take the Club Back to at Least Level to the Ground on the Backswing, or
Point the Club at the Target at the Top of the Backswing

I dislike the notion of *placing* the club anywhere. Many golfers who go along with this idea do nothing but drop the club to what they think is the parallel location – parallel to the intended line of flight. They do so, moreover, by using their hands in the absence of body involvement. The consequence is that they generate very little momentum during their backswing; they make, in effect, an artificial backswing.

All the more power to the golfer who can *reach* parallel at the top of his swing; as long as he does so via weight transfer and rotation. This is a true backswing – when the bigger muscles of the body carry the club to its inevitable destination. The club's exact location at the top of the swing is also dependent on a golfer's flexibility. I wouldn't worry about where your club is at the top; concentrate on activating with the lower body and power will surge from the legs through the hips, trunk, upper chest, shoulders, and arms, and out into the clubhead. This is a natural sequence that you set in motion via footwork. Conscious hand action interrupts the pattern and falsifies the backswing.

The golfer who reaches parallel at the top of his swing has not necessarily made an effective swing motion. The appropriate top-of-the-backswing position is a result, not an action, and involuntary, not voluntary. Let the clubhead flow back. Give up control to gain control.

Hold a Platter in the Right Palm at the Top of the Swing, Facing Skyward

This rather captivating image is a variation on the previous theme. The thinking is that if you can hold the platter skyward

you will have reached that supposedly desirable top-of-the-backswing position. We are again told to make something happen. But we will attain this position, or close to it, if we simply allow the club to flow back on its own, governed as always by balance, weight transfer, and trunk rotation.

Hold a Handkerchief Under Right Arm Pit (or Left Arm Pit)

Here's one that could do some damage. The theory is that by holding the handkerchief you will keep your arms in close to

your body during the swing. The natural golf swing is one in which you don't focus on the precise location of your arms. If you set up well and incorporate the principles of weight transfer and rotation, your arms will swing back on track. They can't do otherwise if you don't interfere. You've arranged the path during the starting position and established it by your motion.

Cock the Wrists (Wherever)

We're told to set the angle early, that is, break our wrists as soon as we start our backswing. Then we're to retain that angle between the wrists and the club-head until just before impact, when we are to consciously let our wrists uncock. Or else we're advised to cock the wrists at the top of the swing, or as soon as we begin our downswing. The common theme is that we must *do something* that is a by-the-way, involuntary happening.

We've seen that the wrists cock on their own as we swing back and through. To add wrist cock is to exaggerate. We also influence the plane and arc by adding wrist cock. The damage done to the natural swing is irreparable. Remember the rule: we do nothing at the expense of balance. Cocking the wrists is an out-of-balance condition.

Keep the Right Elbow Pointing Downward

The golfer who concentrates on any single position during the swing is likely to exaggerate that position. Emphasis on the placement of the right elbow during the swing is an interference that will throw the club off-plane. You will also destroy your arc.

The transfer of weight and trunk rotation will generate a natural folding of the right elbow during the backswing. Maximum extension will ensure that the elbow is in its correct and most useful position.

Pull the Church Bell to Start the Downswing

Here's one that makes golfers think they have found a genuine secret to the game. It also makes them crazy, since it's based on a misperception of an effect of the downswing when we transfer weight from the right foot to the left foot, which drops the downswing plane. It appears that the golfer is pulling the club down as if he were pulling a church bell. It even feels like a pull. That's how it felt to Sam Snead, perhaps *the* natural golfer. He came up with this image. However, we are not pulling. We are being pulled. If you consciously pull, you will destroy your swing plane. We feel the pull because of centrifugal force; the clubhead is pulled outward and downward. The shoulder joints extend because of the force as long as we are relaxed.

The transfer of weight that initiates the unloading motion actually begins when we are still moving back. We've been intent on weight transfer and rotation from our starting positions – they are the motors that drive the motion. At the same time, we are focused on our target. That focus, that intent of moving to our target, is what initiates the downswing. Had we no serious intent of moving to the target, we would have a difficult time knowing when to begin the downswing motion. Given target awareness, however, and given our desire to maintain balance, we will begin the downswing motion when we sense it is time to do so; not to do so would be to fall out of balance. This is a sensory experience that we cannot codify or legislate. I cannot tell you when to begin your downswing motion. I can only tell you that as you become more sensitive to balance you will know when to do so.

Shift Your Weight Laterally to Begin the Downswing
This is a reasonable and popular means of transferring weight to the left side and checking against initiating the downswing with the hands. It's been suggested that the golfer who initiates his downswing with a lateral motion of his hips will begin a chain reaction that will result in a multiplication of power and clubhead speed.

The majority of golfers will find it difficult to time the lateral weight shift with the hips. Furthermore, this is a disturbance

and impediment to balance. As
you now know, I advise beginning the downswing motion with
a transfer of weight from the
right foot onto the left foot.
Some teachers advise us to turn
our hips back to the left, and
hard and quickly enough to
transfer the weight to the left
foot. I believe that the *natural*
movement of transferring weight
from the right to the left foot will
do the job more easily. As long
as we keep our minds on where
we are going we will transfer
weight to the left foot. This will
result in our hips turning out
of the way to the left; it's a natural result rather than a
conscious action that we must
learn; involuntary rather than
voluntary.

The other problem that comes
from concentrating on weight
transfer through lateral shift is
that we begin to worry about
how much lateral shift we are to
impose. We also are prone to
throwing our hips forward while
restricting ourselves elsewhere.
A violent lateral shift can also be
painful.

A suggestion: make a motion
to the top of the backswing. Feel
the weight on your right foot.

Now transfer your weight onto
your left foot. Observe what
happens to your hips. They have
shifted on their own.

Now begin the downswing by
shifting your hips laterally. Notice how strenuous this feels. Do
you also not tend to hold weight
back on your right side?

We want to keep the motion
intact from start to finish. So
allow your weight to go from left
to right and right to left. You'll
be able to repeat your motion
much more often this way.

**Bang Your Left Heel
Onto the Ground to Start the
Downswing**
Unnecessary. Granted, your left
heel will come up as you transfer weight from your left to right
side during the backswing motion, and it will come down
again as you move back to the
left foot on your throughswing.
But banging your left heel will
force you off-plane by pulling
your weight to the inside.

We are looking for maximum
width in the arc without violat-
ing balance. A smooth transition
of weight is the most effective
means of doing so. Think of
transferring the weight back on
to the left foot and you will have
every chance of attaining a stable finish position. You will ruin

your chances of doing so if you initiate the downswing by banging the left heel into the ground.

Pronate and Supinate the Wrists

To pronate is to bend the left hand upward so that the angle between the left wrist and forearm is U- or V-shaped. To supinate is to bend or thrust the wrist forward. Many golfers feel they should pronate the wrists at the beginning of their backswing motion, and supinate the left wrist at impact so that the hands are ahead of the clubhead at impact.

Golfers who feel they must pronate and supinate misinterpret what they see. They observe certain positions and assume that the golfer they are watching has made them happen. But there is neither pronation nor supination in the natural golf swing. Passive hands and wrists generate proper positions on their own. You will see in the "plane control" drill that the toe of the club faces skyward during the loading motion and again faces skyward during the unloading motion. Passive hands have taken the toe to these positions, but the golfer who misinterprets what he sees will think he's observing pronation and supination. The fact is that nothing has happened with the hands and wrists. They have remained in the same formation all the way through the motion.

Finish High

The most enjoyable way to finish the swing is to let yourself finish it. There's no need to contrive a position. The swing motion will take you to the best finishing position, in balance with all your weight on the left foot. You'll be staring at the target in natural elevation. But you won't have invented the position. It will be a logical conclusion to a pure motion. You'll get to the "finish high" position naturally. You won't have to put yourself there.

10. Drills to Develop the Swing Motion

THE FOLLOWING DRILLS are designed to eliminate any unnecessary motion in the swing. They will also introduce you to the weight transfers and rotations. I suggest you practise each one daily for a few minutes. You'll soon be quite comfortable with the motions and will have eliminated much of the excess activity that was present in your swing. You'll realize how economical and efficient the swing motion is. It's the golf swing stripped to its essentials.

THE "HELLO THERE" DRILL

This opening drill will help you develop the sensations involved in transferring weight. It will also help you establish the starting and finishing positions.

Pick a target in a room. Assume the stance of the starting position. The right foot is square or at right angles to the target. Place your left foot slightly outside your shoulder with the foot pointed open about twenty-five degrees to your target. Your weight will be evenly distributed between your feet, that is, fifty-fifty. Your posture is up; you are standing proudly.

You can do this drill with a club, as illustrated, or without one. If you haven't got a club handy, place your hands on your hips. Turn your body to face

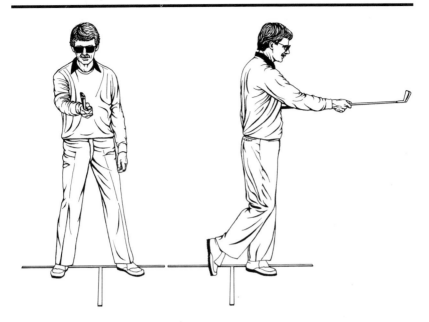

the target. Adjust the position of the left foot until you find a location where you run into a resistance in the left knee and hip which stops your body in a position facing the target. Your right foot will be vertical while your entire body – knees, hips, shoulders, and head – faces the target.

Your objective is to transfer weight from a fifty-fifty distribution at the starting position to one hundred per cent of the body weight on the front foot at the finishing position.

Notice these elements while practising this drill: the slide of your right foot forward; the bend in the right leg to accommodate the weight transfer; the position of the right knee during the finishing position; and the position in which you find you must place your left foot to finish flat on the foot with a hundred per cent of your weight transferred there.

THE "PASSIVE HANDS" DRILL

This drill is designed to eliminate any unnecessary motion in the hands and wrists during the swing motion. It will confirm in your mind that you need only transfer weight to move the clubhead. You will see that the blade angle does remain constant and stable. The drill will establish the fact that you can achieve clubhead control as long as you leave the clubhead alone. Confidence in the clubhead position during the swing breeds the feeling that you can swing freely through the ball toward the target.

Assume the starting position with a golf club in hand. Transfer weight toward your right foot while noticing the clubhead's movement. Continue to transfer weight until the clubhead has moved to shoulder height on the backswing. Allow your hands and wrists to remain passive; that is, let them travel as guided by the lower body motion.

Now transfer weight from the right foot to the left foot until the clubhead has moved to shoulder height on the throughswing. Allow the hands and wrists to remain passive. The feet and legs have moved the clubhead to the desired position. The entire body – knees, hips, chest, shoulders, and head – should be facing the target.

THE "PLANE CONTROL" DRILL

This drill is designed to eliminate any unnecessary rotation of the arms during the swing motion.

Assume the starting form as in the "passive hands" drill. This time move the clubhead to waist height on the backswing, keeping the hands and wrists inactive, or passive. The toe of the club should point skyward. Notice that the means of moving the clubhead was a transfer of weight.

Now transfer the weight and thereby move the clubhead to waist height on the follow-through. Once again, the toe of the club should be facing skyward.

You should be aware of the two weight transfers, the legs and the foot – the footwork – being the means of moving the golf club.

THE "ARM EXTENSION/ ELBOW FOLDING" DRILL

Repeat the "passive hands" drill while maintaining the natural extension of the left arm as in the starting position on the backswing. Remember that the clubhead only travels to shoulder-height.

Now transfer weight to move the clubhead to shoulder-height on the followthrough. Maintain the natural extension of the right arm, as in the starting form.

Notice that the right elbow folds automatically on the backswing, while the left elbow folds automatically on the followthrough; the hands and wrists remain passive.

THE "PENCIL" DRILL

This drill will teach you that there is plenty of room for the shoulders to move as long as you maintain the posture you were in at address.

Place an object such as a pencil between your teeth. Point the pencil in the direction of the ball location or the tee.

Notice the clearance or space between the pencil, the shoulders, and the chin.

Make a swing motion. If the shoulders remain relaxed – that is, hanging naturally – with the head up, the pencil will not interfere with the shoulders, arms, or the chin during the motion. The pencil should be pointing at the target at the completion of the swing motion.

THE "BALL LOCATION" DRILL

We have found a location for
the left foot somewhere outside
the left shoulder so that we will
arrive at the finishing position
in balance with a hundred per
cent of our weight on our left
side. The location of the left foot
is fixed. It's the same for all
shots.

Since the ball is stationary,
we set the club to the ball and
locate ourselves around the club.
The ball and the club become a
unit. Because we are in a balanced form with our arms hanging symmetrically from our body
and the shaft running straight
up and down, bisecting the body,
we find that the ball is just ahead
of the midway point in our stance
for a five-iron shot. The ball
location relative to the left foot
is the same every time. We move
the right foot up and down depending on the width of stance
required for each club. The result is that as the club gets longer
– a two-iron, for example, rather
than a five-iron – the ball will
be further ahead of the midpoint
in your stance because you have
moved your right foot back.
But its location relative to your
left foot will not have changed.

Now we look for the proper distance to stand from the ball. This will differ for every golfer depending upon flexibility. Simply move your body toward or away from the ball until you have found the location where you can make solid contact.

It might appear that this discussion repeats the section on ball location from chapter five, The Starting Form. But it's important that you understand how to place yourself relative to the ball. Practise the proper position on the range and when you have a spare minute or two on the course.

11. The Natural Swing Motion Revisited

THE GOLF SWING can and should be simple. Executed properly, it is relaxing while physically challenging, pleasurable while mentally stimulating.

Every person can play to his potential if he understands the concept of the natural swing motion. The task is to then apply the knowledge in practice in order to develop a repeating, efficient swing. The learning process is as follows: you study the theory of the natural swing motion so that you can understand the fundamentals. As you practise the fundamentals that relate to the theory, you begin to trust yourself. You begin to let go and become more secure because you are working from a logical base. You then begin to enjoy golf much more. You realize that the game does not have to be complicated.

Change is difficult for many people. I know that. We all hang on to what we have learned. But I hope you now understand the concept of the natural golf swing. This understanding, and your ability to evaluate the starting and finishing forms, will enable you to improve day after day. You will find that the deeper your understanding, the

more likely it is that your old habits will fall away. You won't need them anymore. You are now capable of rationally assessing any of your misconceptions about the swing.

I don't want to underestimate the difficulty of change. This is why I ask that you let yourself be freed of the past *gradually*. Remember that you have probably played for years going from one tip to another. Your tendency, no doubt, is to give up on a new tip as soon as you hit a bad shot. You may find that you have the same tendency here. But remember: change that lasts takes time.

The natural swing motion is not a new tip or a quick fix. It is an overall view of the swing that is based on fundamental laws of motion and on fundamental considerations in any physical activity. While I don't believe there's a hole in the theory, that doesn't mean I have all the answers. But I will say

that I have talked with golf professionals all across North America and quizzed biomechanics experts and physicists about the theory. As yet I haven't found any reason to believe the theory is lacking in any way.

Now that I've taken you through the general theory and the segments into which we can break it up, I'd like to describe it as concisely as I can. What I have to say might not have been clear to you at the beginning of the book. But it will now.

The golf swing motion is a natural happening based on a logical sequence of events according to physical laws of centrifugal force and inertia, and performed under the condition and protection of balance. We pre-set in the starting form the circumstances that will allow us to make a pure swing motion toward a target.

The objective is to create a swing motion that has a maximum arc and a true plane. Centrifugal force creates a maximum arc while inertia creates a true plane.

Arc is the perimeter of the swing motion, as defined by the path of the clubhead. In order to maximize the arc and therefore ensure that we can repeat it every time, we maintain elevation and posture throughout the motion. At the same time, centrifugal force creates extension. The result is a maximum arc.

We put the mass – hands, arms, and club – in motion through a weight transfer to our right foot. We allow ourselves to rotate around the trunk of the body to load and then reverse the process to unload and take us to the finishing form.

When we put the mass in motion, it flows on the same path unless disturbed by an outside force. The golfer is in balance from the start and is holding the club – he is really caressing the grip rather than holding it – with a natural extension. Inertia takes over so that the mass travels a pure path, or plane. The flow of the mass changes direction as a result of a weight transfer to the finish. Again it is uninterrupted. We arrive at the finishing position in immaculate balance, facing the target.

The swing motion is a whole-body motion. You can now appreciate that every aspect of the motion is related to every other aspect. I could describe the motion from the point of view of the arc, for example, and show that by arranging for a maximum arc we also design the conditions for weight transfer. That is, we could not produce a maximum arc unless weight transfer were the means of moving the club. If we initiated the motion by picking up the club instead of transferring weight, we would compromise the integrity of the arc. It would shrivel, become smaller and choppier, not a genuine arc at all.

Similarly, I could describe the motion from the perspective of good posture. If we allow ourselves to get out of posture, we change the arc; and of course we also alter the plane. The natural swing motion, then, operates as a feedback loop. Every element can be the central point from which we discuss the motion. Balance is *the* central fundamental.

For interest's sake, let's examine the motion from the point of view of clubhead control. It's fair to say that if we are confident that the clubhead is moving properly, then we will allow ourselves to make the motion. Golfers who try to control the clubhead by manipulating it destroy all other components of the motion. We want to set up a situation so that we need not worry about the clubhead because we know it is flowing properly.

The best swing is one that is uninhibited while under the control that ensues naturally from balance. It is set in motion from a starting position that gives the golfer the best chance to make *his* best motion, considering his physical make-up. The golfer's starting form is one in which he is standing tall. His head rests comfortably – neither up nor down – as he stands proud. His shoulders will have room to move under his chin during the loading motion. He is in good balance, meaning that he is in place, weight evenly distributed between his feet.

Having bent slightly to complete his starting form, he will find that his spine is in its natural state. He is now in a position to swing without restriction. The energy is beginning to flow through his body because he is in a form where he feels free and directed.

The golfer feels directed, of course, because he is aligned to his target properly. His clubface points to the target while his right foot is placed at right angles to it. The left foot is set at least twenty-five degrees open relative to his target, and outside his left shoulder. He intends to transfer his weight during the unloading motion to his left foot, stopping his body directly on the target.

The golfer grips the club lightly, with his arms hanging naturally from his body; they form a spoke or paddle with the club when fully relaxed and extended. The palms of his hands oppose one another.

The relationship of the golfer's arms and hands to the club does not change during the motion. This is "passive hands" and is

further achieved through maximum extension of the arms; relaxed arms are extended arms. If the hands are passive (no conscious activity during the motion), then the clubhead can neither flutter nor waver. And if the golfer makes his motion while maintaining the relationship set up in the starting form, always extended naturally, he will achieve his best, maximum arc. He will generate tremendous power through centrifugal force. All parts will be unified and all parts will respond to the force.

The path of the clubhead relative to the target creates the flight of the ball. The path is set up by the golfer's alignment at address. When a golfer wishes to play a straight shot, he aligns himself square to his target – or as square as he can, given his physical make-up. Should he wish to fade the ball, he will set up open, moving the right foot forward, or toward a line drawn from the ball to the target. And if he wishes to draw the ball, he will set up closed, drawing the right foot back, away from a line drawn from the ball to the target. The tilt of his body will still describe a straight line. The club, swung under conditions of maximum extension, will merely follow that line.

The golfer is now prepared to initiate the motion. His posture is good and will remain so, *tall*, with his spine straight. He is alert and ready. He is full of purpose and is thinking of his objective: to make a swing motion so that he will reach the finishing form he visualizes in his mind's eye.

The golfer initiates the swing motion by transferring weight back to his right foot as his body turns. His left arm and club form a straight line as they extend naturally under the guidance of the transfer and rotation, stretched also by centrifugal force. The clubhead is in perfect control – without the golfer doing anything consciously to make it so – because of inertia. As the golfer reaches his maximum extension during the loading motion, his right arm folds at the elbow. These are all natural happenings.

As the golfer reaches the conclusion of his loading motion, he feels secure. He is swinging without restriction. He knows where the clubhead is because he is aware that he has maintained the blade angle throughout. The natural swing has done it for him. He intends to let the clubhead flow as it will during the unloading motion. His only commitment is to transfer his weight to his left foot and to flow on through to face the target in his finishing form.

The golfer begins the unloading motion by transferring weight to his left foot. This weight shift or reverse sets up clubhead delay and ensures maximum extension at impact as centrifugal force pulls the clubhead outward and downward. This reverse is often mistaken as hand action. It's not. The clubhead is being pulled through the ball by the centrifugal force that has been set up by the weight transfer.

Throughout the unloading motion the golfer is maintaining the posture that he started with. His right arm straightens naturally through impact and his left arm folds beyond impact and on the way to the finish. His hands and wrists remain passive.

This fully coordinated, natural swing motion allows the knees, hips, shoulders, and head to flow through to the finish. They are all facing the target as the golfer arrives in his finishing form. The weight is one hundred per cent on the left foot. The golfer feels an exhilarating sensation of release because the energy he loaded up on when he initiated the motion has now been fully unloaded. He has made a swing motion in balance from start to finish, and has arrived in balance, staring at the target. He has made a natural swing motion.

Glossary

Alignment: body position relative to a specific target.

Arc: circumference or breadth of the swing; a source of power.

Balance: being grounded, secure; mental, physical, and emotional stability.

Centrifugal force: outward force acting on a body that is rotating around a central point.

Clubhead control: created through passive hands and relationship of clubhead to body; also influenced by creating a pure plane and maximum arc.

Conception: theory of the natural swing as motion comprising an arc and plane governed by balance.

Concentration: dealing with the present; comes about through knowledge which eliminates anxiety and fear; elimination of past and future.

Coordination: a unified, complete motion; a flowing connection between segments.

Evaluation: examining the starting and finishing forms.

Extension: enlargement.

Finishing form: knees, hips, shoulders, and head facing target, in balance and full height.

Grip: connection between body and club.

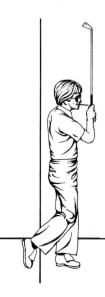

Inertia: property of an object that enables it once set in motion to continue in a state of uniform motion unless otherwise disturbed by an outside force.

Involuntary: positions or actions that happen as a result of the motion; for instance, the clubface returns square to the target line at impact as a result of weight transfer to the finish position. It is a by-the-way, incidental happening that results from the golfer having assumed proper forms and initiating certain actions.

Loading: shifting weight to the right foot and rotating round trunk of body during the backswing motion.

Motion: fluidity of the swing created through weight transfer and rotation.

Passive hands: inactive, quiet, simply holding on to the club and travelling along with the body.

Pivot points: the right and left feet.

Plane: path of the clubhead as created by alignment toward a specific target.

Posture: attitude of the body and mind in balance.

Power: the energy created and released through the swing motion.

Procedure: going through checkpoints in the starting and finishing forms.

Rotation: the motion that necessarily takes place when we load and unload; around the trunk.

Security: the feeling that comes from an understanding of concept, procedure, and evaluation.

Target awareness: clear visualization of the target.

Unloading: weight transfer and rotation during the downswing and throughswing.

Voluntary: skills to be learned; for instance, initiating the swing motion through weight transfer.

Weight transfer: motion to the right foot during the loading motion and to the left foot during the unloading motion.

A Tribute to
George Knudson
1937–1989

G EORGE KNUDSON and I started writing this book in June 1987. George's objective was to help people enjoy golf. He wanted to present them with a logical approach to the swing, so that they could improve their game in the long run. He wanted people to realize their potential.

Soon after we began the book I went to San Francisco to cover the United States Open for *The Globe and Mail*. When I returned a couple of weeks later I learned that George had lung cancer. George knew the prognosis wasn't favourable, but he felt characteristically optimistic. "We'll just work hard on the book," he told me, "and when I have my down days, we'll just wait those out. But we'll get the book done."

We got the book done, and the first printing in hardcover soon sold out. This gratified George, of course, and he deserved the many generous comments that came his way. One fellow in New Orleans, who had watched George play the U.S. tour years before, wrote that George had helped him understand the swing – finally. A young professional in British Columbia quickly knocked three or four shots off his game and looked forward to trying for his tour card. George took this all in stride, as he went through the chemotherapy and radiation treatments that were a part of his life with cancer. He was glad that he had made the game simpler for his readers. He smiled through his pain when he read the letters. I knew how much he was suffering; getting out of bed was as arduous as running a marathon. But he didn't complain.

George died in January 1989. He suffered in his last days, and yet . . . there was that smile. So often he looked up from under his blankets, tired, hurting, and somehow, smiling. Always a wave of the hand when a friend came in, always a hand to clasp the hand of his beautiful wife, Shirley. Shirley: caring, there every day, making George as comfortable as possible, taking him home on weekends, where their three sons Kevin, Paul, and Dean helped. If one can judge a man by his family, especially by the children he has helped raise, then it's fair to say that George was top-class. He was, as the English might say, over the moon with love for his family. George never stopped caring and never stopped showing his love, no matter how much he suffered. He gave and he gave – through his book, through his words, through his actions, through his gestures and the looks on his face.

George loved to strike the golf ball, and to try and understand the swing. Hence his lifelong study of technique. Hence his teaching, which he started in the late 1970s after leaving the tour. Hence this book. He was a perfectionist, a golfer who didn't like to play a round of golf without practising beforehand for at least thirty minutes. One summer evening when George was about fourteen or fifteen his pals at the St. Charles Country Club in Winnipeg convinced him to go out for a few holes. He hadn't practised, but out he went. George hit his first tee shot off the heel of his driver, told his friends "see you later," and went back to the practice tee. Skipping practice meant he hadn't given himself a chance to play his best. What was the point?

Even then George knew what it took to achieve results. And achieve them he did. Ben Hogan said he had the best swing of his generation. Lee Trevino said that George "was one of the greatest ball strikers I've ever seen. If George Knudson had been the putter that [Tom] Watson or I was, or any of the other guys, hell, George Knudson would have won every tournament he ever played in. . . . George Knudson was fantastic when it came to striking golf balls."

But George was much more than a golfer to me. Sure, I would go a long way to watch him hit balls, and was privileged to play with him from time to time. As I write now, I think of his enthusiasm for life, the pleasure he took at being alive, even when there wasn't much life left in him. But I think most of what our friendship has meant.

Before I knew George well – long before – he helped me. I wrote my first article for a major magazine in 1979, just a short time after we met. George read it. He was on the phone that evening. "Lorne," he told me, "you've got your foot in the door. Just keep writing and good things will happen." That sort of generosity was typical of George.

George's own dream was someday to live in the country and paint. He enjoyed painting, and had studied art in Winnipeg before he took up golf. I remember walking into his home in north Toronto the first time and thinking that here was the home of an artist. There was a view, open spaces, trees, nature's gifts to which George responded so completely. We spent many happy times on the back patio by the pool, overlooking the Don Valley ravine, while we worked on this book. George was in his element. He helped me appreciate what was so special about golf – that it was a place to quiet the mind. And he encouraged me to keep my mind as quiet as possible. He told me that if I liked golf – the freedom, the sense of escape, the healthy air – then I would also like skiing. He knew that peace of mind was rare, and important. And if I could have more of it, through golf, through skiing, whatever, I should go for it. That was George all the way.

I remember one evening when I visited George in the hospital. We talked quite late into the night. He told me that if he were to build his own course it wouldn't have any in-course out-of-bounds. "The general feeling would be that of freedom," he said. And he spoke about how aware he was feeling now, even more aware than he had felt when well – and he was plenty aware then. He recalled being on a golf course and being so tuned in to his surroundings that he could see a drop of water glistening on a branch of a nearby willow tree. He was weak, and spoke softly. But there was no mistaking the conviction in his voice.

"I want people to come alive," he said to me late that winter night. "I want them to use all their senses. That's what I'm all about."

That's what George was about all right. No doubt about it. He loved life, the uncomplicated thrill of a cleanly-hit iron shot, the sun over the ocean surrounding the sixteenth green at Cypress Point in California, his favourite course, evenings in ski country north of Toronto, his friends and family gathered round. His mind and his eyes and his heart were open. He helped me open my senses, and he was a true friend.

Lorne Rubenstein
January 1989